The Prevention of Sui

Suicide is considered to be the leading cause of preventable death in prisons. While there is increasingly expansive literature examining the various risk factors associated with a likelihood of eventual prison suicide, so far this has struggled to lead to successful prevention programmes. An alternative approach is needed that seeks to understand, at the individual level, what leads a prisoner to contemplate ending their own life. This book describes how the authors developed and delivered evidence-based psychological interventions for suicide prevention in prison.

The authors present a compelling argument for a psychological approach to the prevention of prison suicide, drawing upon a cognitive behavioural perspective, with chapters investigating two novel psychological therapies: Cognitive Behavioural Suicide Prevention and problem-solving training. The methodology behind each study is presented alongside preliminary findings emerging from the evaluations, and detailed case studies are included as exemplars of the process and content of the therapies, as well as the individual and contextual challenges to be overcome. The book provides timely research into the development of a better understanding of why prisoners engage in suicide behaviour and the preventive interventions showing the most promise for future investigation.

The Prevention of Suicide in Prison will be critical reading for clinical and forensic psychologists, psychological therapists, psychiatrists and other mental health staff working within a prison context, as well as postgraduates in training and researchers studying suicide in forensic settings.

Daniel Pratt is Lecturer in Clinical Psychology at Manchester University, UK, and a Clinical Psychologist at the Manchester Mental Health and Social Care Trust (MMHSCT), UK.

Advances in Mental Health Research Series

Books in this series:

The Clinical Effectiveness of Neurolinguistic Programming
A critical appraisal
Edited by Lisa Wake, Richard M. Gray & Frank S. Bourke

Group Therapy for Adults with Severe Mental Illness
Adapting the Tavistock Method
Diana Semmelhack, Larry Ende & Clive Hazell

Narratives of Art Practice and Mental Wellbeing
Reparation and connection
Olivia Sagan

Video and Filmmaking as Psychotherapy
Research and practice
*Edited by Joshua L. Cohen and J. Lauren Johnson
with Penelope P. Orr*

Schizotypy
New dimensions
Edited by Oliver Mason and Gordon Claridge

The Prevention of Suicide in Prison
Cognitive behavioural approaches
Edited by Daniel Pratt

The Prevention of Suicide in Prison

Cognitive behavioural approaches

Edited by Daniel Pratt

Routledge
Taylor & Francis Group

LONDON AND NEW YORK

First published 2016
by Routledge

2 Park Square, Milton Park, Abingdon, Oxfordshire OX14 4RN
711 Third Avenue, New York, NY 10017

Routledge is an imprint of the Taylor & Francis Group, an informa business

First issued in paperback 2017

British Library Cataloguing in Publication Data
A catalogue record for this book is available from the British Library

Library of Congress Cataloging-in-Publication Data
The prevention of suicide in prison : cognitive behavioural approaches /
    edited by Daniel Pratt.
      pages cm
    Includes bibliographical references and index.
 1. Prisoners—Suicidal behavior.   2. Suicide—Prevention.
3. Prisoners—Psychology.   I. Pratt, Daniel, 1973– editor.
    HV6545.6.P744 2015
    365′.6672—dc23
    2015010433

ISBN: 978-0-415-72460-9 (hbk)
ISBN: 978-0-8153-5769-8 (pbk)

Typeset in Times New Roman
by Apex CoVantage, LLC

The vilest deeds like poison weeds,
    Bloom well in prison-air:
It is only what is good in Man
That wastes and withers there:
Pale Anguish keeps the heavy gate,
    And the Warder is Despair.

(from 'The Ballad of Reading Gaol',
Oscar Wilde, 1898)

Contents

List of tables and figures   ix
Notes on contributors   xi

1   **Suicide in prisons: introducing the problems**   1
    DANIEL PRATT

2   **The epidemiology of prison suicide**   19
    DANIEL PRATT

3   **Psychological models of suicidal ideation and
    behaviour**   35
    PATRICIA GOODING AND DANIEL PRATT

4   **Cognitive behaviour therapy for suicidal prisoners**   49
    DANIEL PRATT

5   **Problem-solving training for suicidal prisoners**   69
    AMANDA PERRY, MITCH WATERMAN AND ALLAN HOUSE

6   **Forensic patient and public involvement: the development
    and maintenance of an ex-offender service user
    reference group**   85
    YVONNE AWENAT

7   **Overcoming the challenges of implementing psychological
    interventions for the prevention of suicide in a
    prison setting**   103
    DANIEL PRATT

8   **Improving the delivery of psychological therapy within
     a male high-security prison: a qualitative enquiry**   115
     FIONA ULPH

9   **Concluding reflections**   133
     DANIEL PRATT

     Index   145

List of tables and figures

Tables

1.1   Numbers and rates of male prisoner suicide in 12 countries
      for 2003–2007   7
1.2   Number and rate of suicide, per 100,000, in US local jails
      and state prisons, 2000–2011   10

Figures

1.1   Total number and rate per 100,000 prisoners of self-inflicted
      death (SID) for prisons in England and Wales, from
      1978–2013   8
3.1   Interaction of entrapment and coping skills on the prediction
      of suicide probability hopelessness   43
3.2   Interaction of defeat and coping skills on the prediction of
      suicide probability hopelessness   43
4.1   Formulation for Mark   62
5.1   Forest plot of problem-solving interventions on repetition
      of self-harm   73
8.1   Three groups of participants contributing to the qualitative
      investigation   116

Notes on contributors

Yvonne Awenat is a Research Fellow within the School of Psychological Sciences at the University of Manchester, UK. Her research interests include psychological approaches to understanding suicidality and the role of service user and professional stakeholders in psychological interventions to reduce suicide. As such, Yvonne takes a leading role in Patient and Public Involvement in research and education. Yvonne practices and teaches qualitative research methods and is a grant holder on two suicide prevention studies. Prior to her work in the field of Clinical Psychology, Yvonne had over 25 years' experience as a senior nurse in the NHS. She holds a Directorship with a local branch of Mind, where she is actively involved in developing strategies to improve the lives of people with mental distress.

Patricia Gooding is a Senior Lecturer in the School of Psychological Sciences, University of Manchester, UK, where she has been based for 11 years. She is Director of the Suicide Research Group in the School. Together with Professor Nick Tarrier, Trish developed a contemporary psychological model of suicide called the Schematic Appraisals Models of Suicide, or the SAMS. The Suicide Research Group is assessing the extent to which the SAMS can explain suicidal thoughts and behaviours trans-diagnostically in people with experiences of psychosis, post-traumatic stress disorder, depression and bipolar disorder.

Allan House is Professor of Liaison Psychiatry, University of Leeds, UK. Allan graduated in medicine from St Bartholomew's Hospital in London. He trained in psychiatry in Nottingham and Oxford and in 1989 moved to Leeds to work as a consultant and senior lecturer in liaison psychiatry, based at Leeds General Infirmary. In 1999, he was appointed Professor of Liaison Psychiatry in the School of Medicine in Leeds. Allan's research interests cover a number of aspects of liaison psychiatry – the sub-specialty of psychiatry concerned with practice in non-psychiatric settings. He has published widely in the areas of psychiatric co-morbidity complicating physical illness, unexplained medical presentations and self-harm. Allan currently works in the multi-disciplinary Leeds Institute of Health Sciences, UK.

Amanda Perry is a Chartered Forensic Psychologist and Senior Research Fellow in the Mental Health and Addiction Research Group in the Health Sciences Department at the University of York, UK. Amanda is interested in the application of psychological therapies for dealing with general mental health and addiction problems within criminal justice populations. She specialises in the development of interventions and assessment of self-harm and suicidal behaviour in the prison environment and is implementing a problem-solving skills training program for prison staff who deal with prisoners at risk of self-harm behaviour.

Daniel Pratt is a Lecturer in Clinical Psychology within the School of Psychological Sciences, University of Manchester, UK, and a Chartered Clinical Psychologist for Manchester Mental Health and Social Care NHS Trust, UK. For the past 13 years, Dan has conducted research investigating psychological models of suicidal behaviour with a view to developing effective preventive interventions. He is currently involved in the development and evaluation of a new Cognitive Behavioural Suicide Prevention (CBSP) therapy, which has already been trialled with people experiencing psychosis, high-risk prisoners, and within mental health in-patient services.

Fiona Ulph is a Chartered Health Psychologist, Senior Lecturer in qualitative methods (School of Psychological Sciences, University of Manchester, UK), Senior Advisor in qualitative methods for the UK NIHR North West Research Design Service and Chair of the Manchester Children's Health Psychology Network, UK. Her research focuses on communication and decision making in healthcare settings, though she advises on numerous projects that employ qualitative methods in novel research settings or that seek to include participants whose voices are rarely heard in research.

Mitch Waterman is Pro-Dean for Student Education in the Faculty of Medicine and Health at the University of Leeds, UK. Mitch remains active with research, with a background in neuroscience and, since 2000, forensic psychology; past projects have involved development of objective tests for sexual interests and violence, the experience of drug users in prisons and the co-occurrence of aggression and self-harming behaviour in prison and clinical populations. Current research includes the Sexual Thoughts Project, a large-scale survey of men's sexual thoughts and an NIHR Research for Patient Benefit project exploring problem-solving interventions for prisoners at risk of self-harm in prisons.

1 Suicide in prisons

Introducing the problems

Daniel Pratt

Background

More than 10 million people are currently held in custody across the world, and the numbers of prisoners are increasing in more than 70% of countries (Walmsley, 2013). Around half of the prisoners are contained in the United States (2.24M), China (1.64M) or Russia (0.68M). The proportion of a country's general population held in prison can be referred to as its prison population rate and is calculated per 100,000 of the nation's population. Whilst not regarded as precise, such rates do allow for comparisons across various countries and regions of the world. The United States has the highest prison population rate in the world with 716 prisoners per 100,000 persons, whilst the prison population rate for England and Wales (148 per 100,000) is at the mid-point in the World List and one of the highest rates in the European Union (Walmsley, 2013).

Sykes's (1958) seminal work on prison society brought attention to the 'pains of imprisonment' as deprivations of liberty, autonomy, goods and services, security and heterosexual relationships. The impact of these stressors upon the individual and how effectively the prisoner can manage this impact varies substantially (Toch, 1992). Prisoner suicide can be seen as the most extreme expression of a failure to cope and adapt to the demands, restraints and frustrations of imprisonment. It remains the responsibility of the prison authorities to protect the health, safety and well-being of prisoners, and failure to meet this responsibility can be open to legal challenge (World Health Organization, 2007).

What is suicide?

One of the first problems encountered when researching suicide, in any population, is how best to define what this term actually means. There are a great number of definitions of 'suicide', and the working definition adopted by a study can have a large impact on the findings of the investigation. According to the Oxford English Dictionary, 'suicide' is defined as *"the, or an, act of taking one's own life; self-murder"*. Perhaps one of the most frequently quoted definitions of suicide used in medical research is by Durkheim (1897, p. 42):

> The termination of an individual's life resulting directly or indirectly from a positive or negative act of the victim himself which he knows will produce the fatal result.

However, this definition has been heavily criticised and even described as unworkable (Baechler, 1980). For example most people would be aware that regularly drinking vast amounts of alcohol, injecting heroin and smoking crack cocaine is likely to inflict serious injury, and even death, upon a person. If a death does result from such behaviour, should this be considered to be a suicide?

Farmer (1988) suggested that a death should be declared as 'suicide' only if three sufficient conditions are met:

1   The death must be recognised as unnatural
2   The initiator of the course of action that led to the death has to be recognised as the deceased himself
3   The motive of self-destruction has to be established.

In England and Wales, deaths are declared as 'suicide' according to the verdicts returned at inquest by coroners or their juries, where the coroner or jury is convinced 'beyond reasonable doubt' that the victim's death was self-inflicted and that the deceased intended to end his or her own life. This high standard of proof leads to some deaths not to be declared as 'suicide'. A death may be commonly considered to have been a deliberate and intended attempt to end life, but the absence of sufficient evidence of intent prevents a verdict of suicide. In such circumstances, the self-inflicted death tends to be recorded as an 'open' verdict.

So far, the answer to the question of "What is suicide?" may be seen as apparently straightforward. However, this would be misleading because there has been considerable definitional obfuscation around suicide and suicide-related behaviours for several decades (De Leo, Burgis, Bertolote, Kerkhof, & Bille-Brahe, 2006; Linehan, 2000). The academic literature is "replete with confusing terms, definitions and classifications" (Silverman, Berman, Sanddal, O'Carroll, & Joiner, 2007a, p. 249), such as suicidal ideation, intent, threat, gesture, attempt, parasuicide and completed suicide.

Confusion is particularly common when considering the terms 'self-harm' and 'suicide', because both refer to acts of deliberate self-injury. If we look to the definitions presented earlier in this chapter, for behaviour to be described as related to suicide, there would be an intent or motive for this behaviour to lead to the end of one's own life. Self-harm comprises behaviours with a broader range of motives or reasons which, in addition to suicidal, may also include non-suicidal intentions. For instance, a person's motivation for self-harm may be to show desperation to others, to seek help, to change the behaviours of others or to gain relief from tension (Hawton & James, 2005). There is further potential for confusion when the consequences of self-harm behaviours are considered, because some deaths may result from self-harm even though this outcome was not intended by the individual.

To be clear, within this book, we consider suicide to lie on a cognitive behavioural continuum from thoughts about death and a reluctance to go on living, through suicide ideation, planning, action in the form of attempts, through to a suicidal death. The suicidal individual is not considered to progress along this continuum in a linear fashion but more likely to oscillate across various stages according to his or her changing circumstances and daily experiences. Certain aspects of this continuum may overlap with features of self-harm; however, rather than becoming entangled into a definitional argument, we have taken a more pragmatic view that all aspects of suicide behaviour are in themselves distressing, disruptive and undesirable and, as such, are important targets of preventive intervention (Tarrier et al., 2013).

Rates of suicide in the general population

According to World Health Organization (WHO) estimates, each year approximately one million people die from suicide and 10 or 20 times more people attempt suicide worldwide. This represents one death every 40 seconds and one attempt every 3 seconds. More people are dying from suicide than in all of the several armed conflicts around the world.

In the UK, suicide is the third largest cause of death, accounting for almost 6,000 deaths per year (Office for National Statistics [ONS], 2014). Over the past 60 years, the total number of suicides in the UK has changed little. In 1950, there were 4,660 self-inflicted deaths, and in 2012, this figure was 5,981, an increase of less than 30% in 62 years. Despite slight variation each year, the suicide rate over this time period has steadily remained between 7 and 11 persons per 100,000 persons (ONS, 2014).

The rate of suicide varies widely across and within the different continents of the world. Within some regions of the world, all countries seem to maintain similar rates. For example in the Western Pacific region, which includes Australia, New Zealand, China and Hong Kong, all countries maintain average suicide rates of between 12 and 15 persons per 100,000 per year. In the Americas region, Argentina and Brazil have a similar suicide rate of between 3 and 7 persons per 100,000 per year, and yet Cuba has a rate of over 20 persons per 100,000 per year (http://www.who.int/healthinfo/mortality_data/en/). In Europe, variation across countries is also quite marked. For instance, Denmark has an average rate of over 18 persons per year, much in line with its Scandinavian neighbours. Even higher rates have been observed since 2000 for Russia and many of the former Soviet Republics with rates of more than 40 persons per 100,000 per year. Conversely, the southern European countries of Italy and Greece, have observed much lower suicide rates of less than 7 per 100,000 persons per year.

Diekstra and Garnefski (1995) analysed suicide rates from 1881 to 1988 for 16 European nations by rank ordering according to their national rate of suicide. Whilst each country's suicide rate varied over the 100 year time period, the rank ordering remained relatively constant. One conclusion made from these findings was that suicide rates are determined by persisting cross-national differences including traditions, customs, religions, social attitudes and climate. Durkheim (1897) suggested that suicide rates may be influenced by, amongst other factors, the extent to which individuals are integrated within society. These theories have been extensively researched for more than a century, such that a body of evidence now exists that stresses the importance of social factors such as unemployment, divorce and religion, in explaining national differences and trends in suicide (Gunnell et al., 1999; Lester, 1997).

Investigations into the causes of international differences in suicide rates are beleaguered by varying recording, coding and classification systems (Chishti, Stone, Corcoran, Williamson, & Petridou, 2003). This misclassification bias can be attributed, in part, to the artefacts of death registration (Jougla, Pavillon, De Smedt, & Bonte, 1998). Some countries can register a death as suicide only when a suicide note is left, whilst others require an assessment of suicidal intent. Also, in those countries where suicide is considered socially and culturally unacceptable, the death is more likely to be recorded as 'undetermined', especially in child fatalities (Chishti et al., 2003). It is, however, unlikely that one single factor can be clearly implicated as having sole influence over suicide rates, because the causes of suicide are complex and multi-factorial with all such factors more likely to represent fundamental societal changes (Gunnell, Middleton, Whitley, Dorling, & Frankell, 2003).

What is prison suicide?

Suicide in prisons, jails and other offender facilities has been a long-standing concern for those responsible for the provision of care to prisoners. The first Medical Inspector for Prisons, Dr R. M. Gover, appointed in April 1878 by the Board of Prison Commissioners for England and Wales, considered it 'a matter of urgency' to investigate the apparently large number of suicides in the prisons at that time (Topp, 1979).

As the next chapter will explain in detail, there have been a number of studies describing the characteristics of offenders who complete suicide in jails, prisons and other penal institutions, mostly from the UK (Bogue & Power, 1995; Dooley, 1990; Humber, Webb, Piper, Appleby, & Shaw, 2013; Shaw, Baker, Hunt, Moloney, & Appleby, 2004), North America (Hayes, 1983; Hayes & Rowan, 1988; Winter, 2003) and Australia (Dalton, 1999). However, comparisons of findings from these studies are made difficult by a variety of definitions of suicide and methods used in data collection, as well as the differences in structures of countries' prison systems.

In the UK, the prison services are the responsibility of the central governments with the majority of establishments housing both remand and sentenced prisoners. This is also true for the prison systems of Australia and New Zealand. In the US, a tiered correctional system is employed, whereby local, city or county authorities operate 'jails' that hold offenders on remand or who have received shorter sentences of, typically, less than one year. State or federal 'prisons' house offenders who have received longer sentences. The Canadian prison system is also tiered and similar to that in the US. State jails house offenders on remand or serving shorter sentences and federal penitentiaries contain offenders serving longer sentences usually of more than two years.

In addition to the varying structures of countries' prison systems, research into prison suicide has also been 'bedevilled' by definitional problems (Felthous, 2011; McHugh & Towl, 1997). First, the term 'self-inflicted death' (SID), currently used by Her Majesty's Prison Service in the UK to refer to all apparent suicides in custody, was adopted in 1991 as an all-embracing definition of deaths arising from non-natural causes that appeared to be directly caused by the actions of the individual concerned (Snow, Paton, Oram, & Teers, 2002). Therefore, SIDs in custody include coroner's verdicts of suicide, open verdicts, deaths by misadventure and accidental deaths (Snow & McHugh, 2002). As for investigations of suicide in the general population, many studies of prisoner suicide also include open verdicts in recognition that a reliance on recorded verdicts of suicide alone often leads to under-recording of suicidal deaths because open verdicts are often cases of suicide that were not or could not be proven by the coroner. However, HM Prison Service's definition of SID, which includes suicide, open verdicts, deaths by misadventure and accidental deaths results in SID rates that are likely to be over-estimates of the true rate of suicide reported by most empirical investigations.

Another definitional problem when researching suicide in prisons relates to the calculation of the rate of suicide amongst prisoners, specifically with respect to the denominator used in the rate calculations. The most frequently used denominator is the average daily population (ADP) of inmates. However, many prisoners do not stay for a 12-month period so the ADP will under-represent the number of people passing through the prison system; for example in 2000, the ADP was 64,602 prisoners, although there were 129,733 receptions coming into prisons (Sattar, 2001). Also, suicide rates calculated using ADP figures have been shown to over-estimate the true rates, especially amongst remand prisoners. Towl & Crighton (1998) reported a suicide rate in remand prisoners of 238 per 100,000 per year using ADP figures that fell to 39 per 100,000 per year when calculated using remand reception figures.

To calculate the annual rates of suicide in prisons more accurately, we would need to obtain the number of persons imprisoned for each year and the length of time each person spent in custody. Unfortunately, such detailed data are not readily available. Therefore, despite these problems of under-representation and over-estimation, rates calculated using ADP figures are most frequently quoted, enabling researchers to make fair comparisons with previous work and also across different countries and regions of the world.

A further difficulty to be addressed when reporting accurate rates of prison suicide relates to the stigma and perceived consequences of the occurrence of a death in custody. The responsibility for ensuring the health and well-being of prisoners rests with the prison institution and a death in custody can indicate a clear failure to meet this responsibility. Previous reports have highlighted the cover-up and misclassification of prison suicides (Liebling, 1994; Smith, 1984) to avoid unwanted attention upon the staff and procedures of the host institution and to reduce the threat of litigation. Accurate reporting of suicidal deaths in custody may present a conflict in interest for the prison authority.

Rates of suicide in prisoner populations

Suicides rates in prison are substantially higher than in the general population, with the prison population typically associated with an up to tenfold increase in risk (Fazel, Grann, Kling, & Hawton, 2011). In the UK, suicide rates are approximately 5 times greater for males (Fazel, Benning, &

Danesh, 2005) and 20 times greater for females in prison (Fazel & Benning, 2009). Figure 1.1 displays the total number and rate per 100,000 of SID within prisons in England and Wales, from 1978 through to 2013. We can see a marked increase in the rate of SID over the past 35 years. The average SID rate per year for the early 1980s remained at 60 rising to over 130 by the start of the 21st century. There have also been significant fluctuations over this period. The largest increase in the SID rate, in a single year, was between 1986 and 1987, where the rate more than doubled from 45 to 95 deaths per 100,000 per year. Other notable single year increases can be seen between 2001–2002 (22%), 2006–2007 (36%) and 2012–2013 (29%). Despite the fluctuations in this data, an upward trend is clearly discernible (Sedenu, 2005; Snow et al., 2002).

Whilst prison population figures for almost all countries are routinely calculated and collated by the United Nations, the same cannot be said for numbers and rates of suicide or self-inflicted deaths in prisons. For those countries where rates have been calculated, this work is usually to be found amongst the academic literature as opposed to in official reports. For this reason, comparisons of rates are compromised by the lack of available data for most countries, especially in the non-Westernised world. Countries adopt a variety of definitions of SID and a number of different methods of recording prison populations. This makes it difficult to draw firm conclusions from any international comparisons. One of the few international investigations of prison suicide was conducted by Fazel et al. (2011), who described the numbers and rates of prison suicide in 12 countries during 2003–2007 (see Table 1.1 for male suicides).

Table 1.1 Numbers and rates of male prisoner suicide in 12 countries for 2003–2007 (derived from Fazel et al., 2011)

Country	Number of prison suicides	Suicide rate per 100,000 prisoners
Australia	69	58
Belgium	50	109
Canada	44	70
Denmark	29	147
England and Wales	384	107
Finland	17	96
Ireland	10	64
The Netherlands	84	108
New Zealand	24	67
Norway	19	127
Scotland	40	117
Sweden	40	128

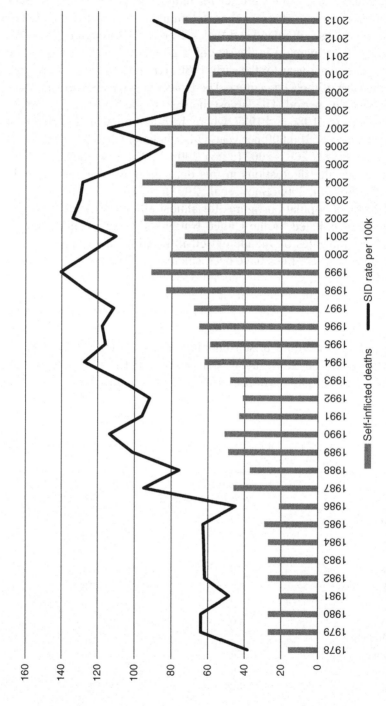

Figure 1.1 Total number and rate per 100,000 prisoners of self-inflicted death (SID) for prisons in England and Wales, from 1978–2013 (derived from www.gov.uk/government/collections/safety-in-custody-statistics, Ministry of Justice, 2014)

We can see that the prison suicide rate of 107 per 100,000 prisoners, placed England and Wales 'mid-table' compared with other European countries, with the Scandinavian countries experiencing the highest rates. Compared with the general population, the relative rates of prison suicide suggested a three- to eightfold increase in risk amongst prisoners.

Outside of Europe there is little comparable data on a national level to draw upon, despite various studies reporting rates of SID amongst prisoners. This data often pertain to various date ranges and usually on prison populations of a specific region rather than on a nation as a whole. This latter fact is especially true for data from the US. Comparisons with the US are further complicated by the various types of correctional facilities, each with its own distinct eligibility criteria. Suicide rates for US 'jails', which usually house persons awaiting trial or serving short sentences, tend to be significantly higher than for US 'prisons', which house inmates serving sentences of more than one year (Hayes & Blaauw, 1997).

As can be seen in Table 1.2, the number and rate of suicide in local jails in the US has consistently been greater than for state prisons (US Department of Justice and Bureau of Justice Statistics, 2013). It is also clear that the rate for jails is consistently around 40 per 100,000, whilst the rate for prisons is around 15 per 100,000. This compared with a suicide rate for the US general population of approximately 12 per 100,000 (Centers for Disease Control and Prevention, 2014). The national figures by the Office of Justice Programs, US Department of Justice, fail to reveal the substantial variability within suicide rates across the different states of the US. In a review, Hayes (1995) reported prison suicide rates ranged from 19 per 100,000 in Texas through to 54 per 100,000 in the Oregon prison system. It must be noted in such comparisons that most of the studies included in the review provided suicide rates that pertained to different time periods and, as we have already seen for UK prisons, suicide rates do vary widely from year to year.

A similar infrastructure to the US penal system also exists in Canada, which has provincial prisons, housing people sentenced to less than two years, and federal penitentiaries, for prisoners with sentences of two or more years. Wobeser, Datema, Bechard, & Ford, (2002) identified 90 suicides in a study of the causes of death among people in custody in Ontario. This produced suicide rates of 68 per 100,000 inmates in provincial prisons and 103 per 100,000 in federal penitentiaries.

More national data are available for Australian prisons because the Australian Institute of Criminology maintains the National Deaths in Custody database, which stores information on the incidence and nature of all deaths occurring in all custodial settings in Australia (Collins & Mouzas,

Table 1.2 Number and rate of suicide, per 100,000, in US local jails and state prisons, 2000–2011 (derived from US Department of Justice and Bureau of Justice Statistics, 2013)

		2000	2001	2002	2003	2004	2005	2006	2007	2008	2009	2010	2011
Local jails	No. of suicides	289	313	314	296	299	286	278	284	228	304	305	310
	Suicide rate	48	49	47	43	42	39	36	36	29	41	42	43
State prisons	No. of suicides		168	168	199	199	213	219	215	197	202	215	185
	Suicide rate		14	14	16	16	17	17	16	15	15	16	14

2002). Between 1980 and 2001, a total of 966 people died in prison custody in Australia, of which 458 (47%) were attributed to suicide, yielding an annual rate of prison suicide of 147 per 100,000 inmates. In a comparison of the rates of suicide in Australian prisons with the general population, between 1980 and 1998 Dalton (1999) found that the rate of suicide in the general population of Australia increased by 39% compared with an increase of over 75% in the suicide rate in Australian prisons.

How do prisons prevent suicide?

Suicidal behaviour in prisons may be conceptualised as an interaction of vulnerability that prisoners import from society into the establishments and the deprivation endured by the prisoner whilst in custody (Kerkhof & Bernasco, 1990; Liebling, 1992). Recognising the importance of this interaction of the vulnerable individual with a challenging environment, suicide prevention in prisons tends to be categorised into primary and secondary strategies. Primary strategies target environmental factors that could have an effect on the overall incidence of suicide in prisons, for example policies and procedures, staffing practices and the physical design of the establishment. Secondary strategies focus on ways to intervene with offenders considered to be at high risk of suicide, for example counselling, peer support and prisoner observation aides (Conacher, 1993). In the UK, HM Prison Service has approached suicide prevention from both the primary and secondary perspectives.

Approaches to the prevention of suicide in prisons are determined by the policies and procedures put in place by the prison authorities and, as such, can vary across jurisdictions in terms of emphasis placed upon specific strategies and interventions. The *International Association for Suicide Prevention Task Force on Suicide in Prisons* proposed several service-level strategies that should be considered to be best practice. This list contained reception screening, comprehensive assessment to enable identification of at-risk individuals, detailing monitoring and observation, staff training, a multi-disciplinary communication and sufficient mental healthcare services (Konrad et al., 2007). Reception screening offers the opportunity to make a timely referral for any clinical need or problem as soon as the individual enters the prison. This opportunity is especially important because many prison suicides occur in the early stages of imprisonment (Fruehwald, Frottier, Matschnig, König, & Bauer, 2004; Towl & Crighton, 1998). Ongoing monitoring and evaluation of at-risk prisoners ensures that all staff working with the prisoner are fully up-to-date on any dynamic stressors and their impact upon the individual's current behaviour

(Konrad et al., 2007). Regular multi-disciplinary meetings allow for the review of the prisoner's risk status and refinement of appropriate care and support interventions recommended to meet his or her needs. This system of risk management would be closely aligned with the institution's mental healthcare services, especially because the majority of suicidal prisoners also experiencing ongoing mental health problems (Fazel, Cartwright, Norman-Nott, & Hawton, 2008). Furthermore, mental health and suicide awareness training of all staff is now routine practice for many countries (Humber, Hayes, Senior, Fahy, & Shaw, 2011).

In the UK, following the publication of a review of suicide and self-harm in prisons by Her Majesty's Chief Inspector of Prisons for England & Wales (1990), HM Prison Service (1994) launched a new strategy for prisoners at risk of suicide entitled 'Caring for the Suicidal in Custody'. Most notably, the prevention of prison suicide passed from a medicalised approach, in which healthcare staff were seen as responsible for identifying and managing prisoners at risk of suicidal behaviour, to a new approach where suicide prevention became the responsibility of every member of prison staff. Suicide Awareness Teams (later subsumed within Safer Custody teams) were introduced in each establishment that were responsible for developing and monitoring a local suicide and self-harm prevention strategy in accordance with the national directive. One of the most important aspects of the strategy was the introduction of case-conferences in providing support to at-risk prisoners (HM Prison Service, 2001). This was underpinned by a Self-Harm at Risk form, which followed the prisoner's every movement to ensure all prison staff had immediate access to risk-pertinent information and support plans that identified and targeted resources to 'at-risk' prisoners. Reviews of this system tended to highlight faults in the implementation of the strategy but recognised the importance of maintaining suicide prevention as a concern for all staff (HM Chief Inspector of Prisons, 1999). The extra responsibility placed upon staff involved in the assessment and management of suicidal prisoners demanded additional support and training to raise staff awareness of suicide and self-injurious behaviour (Howard League for Penal Reform, 2003).

Suicide prevention has remained a high priority for HM Prison Service for more than two decades and, as such, the system to manage suicidal prisoners has been further refined and re-developed during this time. Attempts have been made to more clearly and succinctly describe the procedure and responsibilities required of each grade of staff, and to clarify the use of segregation units to be restricted to exceptional circumstances and for as short a time as possible, and when no other suitable location is appropriate. Furthermore, the use of strip cells and unfurnished cells has been eliminated from the management of suicidal prisoners. Working relationships with third-sector providers (e.g. Samaritans) have been strengthened through the introduction of peer-support schemes. 'Listener' schemes train prisoner volunteers to be able to support their peers during times of crisis, and 'Insider' schemes offer training and guidance to prisoner volunteers who 'buddy' new prisoners at the early stages of custody, a time known to be particularly distressing for many prisoners.

Most recently, the Assessment, Care in Custody and Teamwork (ACCT) initiative introduced a care-planning system operated by multi-disciplinary staff teams to provide individualised care for prisoners at risk of suicidal behaviour (Ministry of Justice, 2013). The ACCT system is similar to the Care Programme Approach used within UK mental healthcare services. The focus of the ACCT procedure has moved away from the surveillance and monitoring of prisoners to a more individualised and interactive process. Aspects of the prisoner's care plan may include increased supervision and observation, increased social support, counselling and special accommodation. ACCT is used both as a crisis intervention and to help prisoners cope with longer term problems.

Investigations and studies to discover what works in prison establishments in the reduction of suicide and self-harming is recognised as a priority for research (Fazel & Lubbe, 2005). To date, several studies have been conducted ranging from discrete evaluations of specific suicide interventions through to longitudinal assessments of how a prison suicide prevention strategy has affected rates of suicide by prisoners. A common theme emerging from this work is the importance of multi-disciplinary working and comprehensive staff training (Humber et al., 2011; Power, Swanson, Luke, Jackson, & Biggam, 2003; Senior et al., 2007; Western Australia Department of Justice Suicide Prevention Taskforce, 2002).

The ACCT system operating within HM Prison Service in England and Wales was subject to a systematic evaluation in five pilot prisons, prior to its full implementation across the prison estate (Humber et al., 2011). In a comparison of the new ACCT system with its predecessor, there was no change in the proportion of suicidal prisoners identified through reception screening. Significantly fewer ACCTs were opened simply on the basis of historical risk, in the absence of current suicidal ideation, suggesting the new system to be more sensitive to current risks. ACCTs were more likely to be opened prior to the occurrence of suicidal behaviour, in response to the presence of potential risk factors such as expression of ideation, unusual behaviour or low mood. This suggests a more pro-active approach was being taken by staff using the ACCT who held a greater awareness of suicidal risks.

In keeping with previous evaluations, the ACCT system has been proven to be successful in the identification and management of prisoners at risk of suicidal behavior; however, the number of open ACCTs in each prison establishment is likely to be an under-estimate of the actual prevalence of suicidality. For example only 1 in 10 prisoners experiencing significant suicidal ideation may be identified within the risk management system by the host prison (Senior et al., 2007). Hence, there remain large proportions of vulnerable prisoners experiencing suicidal distress and not receiving care and support from the institution that holds the responsibility for ensuring their health, safety and well-being.

References

Baechler, J. (1980). *Suicides*. Oxford, UK: Blackwell.

Bogue, J., & Power, K. (1995). Suicide in Scottish prisons, 1976–1993. *Journal of Forensic Psychiatry, 6*(3), 527–540.

Centers for Disease Control and Prevention. (2014). *Web-based injury statistics query and reporting system: Fatal injury reports*. Atlanta, GA: National Center for Injury Prevention and Control. Available from www.cdc.gov/injury/wisqars/index.html

Chishti, P., Stone, D. H., Corcoran, P., Williamson, E., & Petridou, E. (2003). Suicide mortality in the European Union. *European Journal of Public Health, 13*, 108–114.

Collins, L., & Mouzas, J. (2002). Deaths in custody: A gender-specific analysis. *Trends & Issues in Crime and Criminal Justice, no. 238*. Canberra, ACT: Australian Institute of Criminology.

Conacher, G. N. (1993). The issue of suicide in Canadian federal penitentiaries. *Forum on Corrections Research, 5*(1), 25–28.

Dalton, V. (1999). Suicide in prison, 1980 to 1998: A national overview. *Trends & Issues in Crime and Criminal Justice, no. 126*. Canberra, ACT: Australian Institute of Criminology.

De Leo, D., Burgis, S., Bertolote, J. M., Kerkhof, A. J., & Bille-Brahe, U. (2006). Definitions of suicidal behavior. *Crisis: The Journal of Crisis Intervention and Suicide Prevention, 27*(1), 4–15.

Department of Health. (2001). *Safety first: Five-year report of the National Confidential Inquiry into Suicide and Homicide by People with Mental Illness*. London, UK: Author.

Diekstra, R. F., & Garnefski, N. (1995). On the nature, magnitude, and causality of suicidal behaviors: An international perspective. *Suicide and Life-Threatening Behavior, 25*(1), 36–57.

Dooley, E. (1990). Prison suicide in England and Wales, 1972–87. *British Journal of Psychiatry, 156*, 40–45.

Durkheim, E. (1897). *Le Suicide*; Translated in 1952 as *Suicide: A Study in Sociology*, by J. A. Spalding & G. Simpson, London, UK: Routledge and Kegan Paul.

Farmer, R.D.T. (1988). Assessing the epidemiology of suicide and parasuicide. *British Journal of Psychiatry, 153*, 16–20.

Fazel, S., & Benning, R. (2009). Suicides in female prisoners in England and Wales 1978–2004. *British Journal of Psychiatry, 194*, 183–184.

Fazel, S., Benning, R., & Danesh, J. (2005). Suicides in male prisoners in England and Wales 1978–2003. *Lancet, 366*, 1301–1302.

Fazel, S., Cartwright, J., Norman-Nott, A., & Hawton, K. (2008). Suicide in prisoners: A systematic review of risk factors. *Journal of Clinical Psychiatry, 69*(11), 1721–1731.

Fazel, S., Grann, M., Kling, B., & Hawton, K. (2011). Prison suicide in 12 countries: An ecological study of 861 suicides during 2003–2007. *Social Psychiatry and Psychiatric Epidemiology, 46*, 191–195.

Fazel, S., & Lubbe, S. (2005). Prevalence and characteristics of mental disorders in jails and prisons. *Current Opinion in Psychiatry, 18*, 550–554.

Felthous, A.R. (2011). Suicide behind bars: Trends, inconsistencies, and practical implications. *Journal of Forensic Sciences, 56*(6), 1541–1555.

Fruehwald, S., Frottier, P., Matschnig, T., König, F., & Bauer, P. (2004). Suicide in custody: A case-control study, *British Journal of Psychiatry, 185*, 494–498.

Gunnell, D., Lopatatzidis, A., Dorling, D., Wehner, H., Southall, H., & Frankel, S. (1999). Suicide and unemployment in young people. Analysis of trends in England and Wales 1921–1995. *British Journal of Psychiatry, 175*, 263–270.

Gunnell, D., Middleton, N., Whitley, E., Dorling, D., & Frankell, S. (2003). Why are suicide rates rising in young men but falling in the elderly? – A time series analysis of trends in England and Wales 1950–1998. *Social Sciences and Medicine, 57*, 595–611.

Hawton, K., & James, A. (2005). Suicide and deliberate self harm in young people. *British Medical Journal, 330*(7496), 891–894.

Hayes, L.M. (1983). And darkness closes in . . . A national study of jail suicides. *Criminal Justice and Behaviour, 10*(4), 461–484.

Hayes, L.M. (1995). *Prison suicide: An overview and guide to prevention.* Alexandria, VA: National Center on Institutions and Alternatives. Sponsored by National Institute of Corrections, US Department of Justice.

Hayes, L.M., & Blaauw, E. (1997). Prison suicide: A special issue. *Crisis, 18*, 146–147.

Hayes, L.M., & Rowan, J.R. (1988). *National study of jail suicides: Seven years later.* Alexandria, VA: National Center on Institutions and Alternatives. Sponsored by National Institute of Corrections, US Department of Justice.

HM Chief Inspector of Prisons. (1990). *Suicide and self-harm in prison service establishments in England and Wales.* London, UK: HMSO.

HM Chief Inspector of Prisons. (1999). *Suicide is everyone's concern: A thematic review.* London, UK: Home Office.

HM Prison Service. (1994). *Caring for the suicidal in custody.* London, UK: Author.

HM Prison Service. (2001). *Prevention of suicide and self-harm in the prison service: An internal review.* London, UK: Author.

Howard League for Penal Reform. (2003). *Suicide and self-harm prevention: The management of self-injury in prisons.* London, UK: Author.

Humber, N., Hayes, A., Senior, J., Fahy, T., & Shaw, J. (2011). Identifying, monitoring and managing prisoners at risk of self-harm/suicide in England and Wales. *Journal of Forensic Psychiatry & Psychology, 22*(1), 22–51.

Humber, N., Webb, R., Piper, M., Appleby, L., & Shaw, J. (2013). A national case-control study of risk factors among prisoners in England and Wales. *Social Psychiatry and Psychiatric Epidemiology, 48*, 1177–1185.

Jougla, E., Pavillon, F., De Smedt, M., & Bonte J. (1998). Improvement of the quality and comparability of causes of death statistics inside the European Community. *Review Epidemiology Sante Publique, 46,* 447–456.

Kerkhof, J.F.M., & Bernasco, W (1990). Suicidal behaviour in jails and prisons in the Netherlands: Incidence, characteristics, and prevention. *Suicide and Life-Threatening Behavior, 20*(2), 123–137.

Konrad, N., Daigle, M.S., Daniel, A.E., Dear, G.E., Frottier, P., Hayes, L.M., & Sarchiapone, M. (2007). Preventing suicide in prisons, Part 1: Recommendations from the International Association for Suicide Prevention Task Force on Suicide in Prisons. *Crisis, 28,* 113–121.

Lester, D. (1997). An empirical examination of Thomas Masryk's theory of suicide. *Archives of Suicide Research, 3,* 125–131.

Liebling, A. (1992). *Suicides in prison.* London, UK: Routledge.

Liebling, A. (1994). Suicide amongst women prisoners. *The Howard Journal of Criminal Justice, 33*(1), 1–9.

Linehan, M.M. (2000). Behavioral treatments of suicidal behaviors: Definitional obfuscation and treatment outcomes. In R.W. Maris, S.S. Canetto, J.L. McIntosh, & M.M. Silverman (Eds.), *Review of suicidology* (pp. 84–111). New York, NY: Guilford Press.

McHugh, M.J., & Towl, G.J. (1997). Organisational reactions and reflections on suicide and self-injury. In G.J. Towl (Ed.), *Suicide and self-injury in prisons: Issues in criminological and legal psychology, 28* (pp. 5–11). Leicester, UK: British Psychological Society.

Ministry of Justice. (2013). *Management of prisoners at risk of harm to self, to others and from others* (Safer Custody). London, UK: Author.

Ministry of Justice. (2014). *Safety in Custody Statistics England and Wales: Update to December 2013.* London, UK: Author.

O'Donnell, I., & Farmer, R. (1995). The limitations of official suicide statistics. *British Journal of Psychiatry, 166,* 458–461.

Office for National Statistics. (2014). Statistical bulletin: Suicides in the United Kingdom, 2012 Registrations. London, UK: Author.

Power, K., Swanson, V., Luke, R., Jackson, C., & Biggam, F. (2003). *Evaluation of the revised SPS suicide risk management strategy* (Occasional Paper Series 01/2003). Edinburgh, UK: Scottish Prison Service.

Sattar, G. (2001). *Rates and causes of death among prisoners and offenders under community supervision.* London, UK: Home Office.

Sedenu, A. (2005). Safer Custody Group. *British Journal of Forensic Practice, 7*(4), 14–20.

Senior, J., Hayes, A.J., Pratt, D., Thomas, S.D., Fahy, T., Leese, M., . . . Shaw, J.J. (2007). The identification and management of suicide risk in UK prisons. *Journal of Forensic Psychiatry and Psychology, 18*(3), 368–380.

Shaw, J., Baker, D., Hunt, I.M., Moloney, A., & Appleby, L. (2004). Suicide by prisoners: A national clinical survey. *British Journal of Psychiatry, 184,* 263–267.

Silverman, M.M., Berman, A.L., Sanddal, N.D., O'Carroll, P.W., & Joiner, T.E. (2007a). Rebuilding the Tower of Babel: A revised nomenclature for the study of suicide and suicidal behaviors Part 1: Background, rationale, and methodology. *Suicide and Life-Threatening Behavior, 37*(3), 248–263.

Silverman, M.M., Berman, A.L., Sanddal, N.D., O'Carroll, P.W., & Joiner, T.E. (2007b). Rebuilding the Tower of Babel: A revised nomenclature for the study of suicide and suicidal behaviors Part 2: Suicide-related ideations, communications, and behaviors. *Suicide and Life-Threatening Behavior, 37*(3), 264–277.

Smith, R. (1984). The state of the prisons. Deaths in prison. *British Medical Journal* (Clinical Research Ed.), *288*(6412), 208–212.

Snow, L., & McHugh, M. (2002). The aftermath of a death in prison custody. In G.J. Towl, L. Snow, & M. McHugh (Eds.), *Suicide in prisons* (pp. 135–155). Oxford, UK: Blackwell.

Snow, L., Paton, J., Oram, C., & Teers, R. (2002). Self-inflicted deaths during 2001: An analysis of trends. *The British Journal of Forensic Practice, 4*(4), 3–17.

Sykes, G.M. (1958). *The society of captives: A study of a maximum security prison.* Princeton, NJ: Princeton University Press.

Tarrier, N., Gooding, P., Pratt, D., Kelly, J., Awenat, Y., & Maxwell, J. (2013). *Cognitive behavioural prevention of suicide in psychosis: A treatment manual.* London, UK: Routledge.

Toch, H. (1992). *Living in prison: The ecology of survival.* Washington, DC: American Psychological Association.

Topp, D.O. (1979). Suicide in prison. *British Journal of Psychiatry, 134*, 24–27.

Towl, G.J., & Crighton, D.A. (1998). Suicide in prisons in England and Wales from 1988 to 1995. *Criminal Behaviour and Mental Health, 8*, 184–192.

US Department of Justice and Bureau of Justice Statistics. (2013). *Mortality in local jails and state prisons, 2000–2011 – Statistical tables.* Retrieved from www.bjs.gov/content/pub/pdf/mljsp0011.pdf

Walmsley, R. (2013). *World prison population list* (10th ed.). London, UK: International Centre for Prison Studies. Retrieved from www.prisonstudies.org/sites/prisonstudies.org/files/resources/downloads/wppl_10.pdf

Western Australia Department of Justice Suicide Prevention Taskforce. (2002, July 4). *Suicide in prison.* Australia: Author.

Winter, M.M. (2003). County jail suicides in a midwestern state: Moving beyond the use of profiles. *The Prison Journal, 83*(2), 130–148.

Wobeser, W.L., Datema, J., Bechard, B., & Ford, P. (2002). Causes of death among people in custody in Ontario, 1990–1999. *Canadian Medical Association Journal, 167*(10), 1109–1113.

World Health Organization. (1999). *Figures and facts about suicide.* Geneva, Switzerland: Author.

World Health Organization. (2007). *Preventing suicide in jails and prisons.* Geneva, Switzerland: Author.

2 The epidemiology of prison suicide

Daniel Pratt

Background

Suicide has often been established as the single most common cause of preventable death in correctional settings and has been a long-standing concern for those responsible for the provision of care to prisoners. Conducted over several decades, there have been a number of studies describing the characteristics of offenders who complete suicide in jails, prisons and other penal institutions, from the UK (Bogue & Power, 1995; Dooley, 1990; Shaw, Baker, Hunt, Moloney, & Appleby, 2004; Topp, 1979), North America (Hayes, 1983; Hayes & Rowan, 1988) and Australia (Dalton, 1999). Typically, an investigation will collect and collate data on various socio-demographic and clinical characteristics of all suicides that occurred among a specific prisoner group during a specific timescale. A 'suicide profile' can then be developed that highlights the most prevalent features of completed suicides.

Whilst a number of important studies have described the characteristics of those prisoners who have completed suicide in custodial settings, it must be emphasised that such a description does not tell us which of these characteristics are most associated with suicide and could therefore be seen as risk factors. The identification of risk factors for prison suicide requires the inclusion of an adequate control group with which to compare the suicide group. Without the inclusion of a comparison group, it is impossible to know which characteristics are significantly more common amongst suicide victims and which characteristics merely reflect those of the whole prison population from which the suicide group was drawn.

Demographic risk factors

In the community, it has generally been shown that women tend to have consistently lower rates for suicide than men. Because women constitute a very small percentage of the total prison population throughout Western countries (3–7%), it is not surprising that the actual number of suicides by female prisoners is small. However, very few studies provide any specific information on female suicides. The larger descriptive studies of prison suicide have reported between 2% and 8% of deaths were female (Dooley, 1990; Hayes, 1983; Shaw et al., 2004; Towl & Crighton, 1998; Way, Miraglia, Sawyer, Beer, & Eddy, 2005) and so females tend not to be over or under-represented amongst suicides compared with the general prisoner population. More mixed results have been reported by smaller sized descriptive studies; however, small sample sizes tend to lead to less reliable findings. For example a study of 83 suicides on Scottish prisons identified only 1 (1.2%) female, compared with 3% of the Scottish population at the time of the study (Bogue & Power, 1995). Controlled studies of prison suicide, which compare completed suicides with other prisoner groups, add limited support to the suggestion that females are under-represented amongst prisoner suicides. Two separate studies of prisoner suicide in The Netherlands and Austria both reported suicides were no different, with respect to gender, from a comparison group of prisoners (Fruehwald, Frottier, Matschnig, König, & Bauer, 2004; Kerkhof & Bernasco, 1990), whilst a study of US prisoner suicide found females were less likely to complete suicide (Winter, 2003). A resolution of this inconsistency was offered by a controlled meta-analysis of 34 studies of prisoner suicide (Fazel, Cartwright, Norman-Nott, & Hawton, 2008) that identified a disproportionate percentage of male suicides, even when allowing for the fact that the majority of prisoners are male.

Previous studies of prison suicide have tended to highlight prisoner suicides as being older than the general prison population, with the over 30 years age group seen to be at increased risk (Bogue & Power, 1995; Dooley, 1990; Fruehwald et al., 2004; Kerkhof & Bernasco, 1990). However, this finding has not been consistently shown across all prisoner groups, with some contradictory evidence coming from studies of suicides within US jails, where the suicide group were either of a similar age (Winter, 2003) or significantly younger than the general prisoner population (Way et al., 2005).

In the UK, between a quarter and a half of prison suicides were married, with similar figures reported in US and Canadian studies. So it appears that a minority of prison suicides were married at the time of death. However, these proportions may merely reflect those of the prison or jail populations from which the suicide group were drawn. Controlled studies of prisoner suicide in Austria (Fruehwald et al., 2004) and the US (Winter, 2003) failed to identify any significant differences for marital status between suicides and other prisoners. The consideration of 'being married' as offering protection against prisoner suicide may not be as straightforward as first appears. It seems plausible that imprisonment and the possibility of prolonged separation is likely to put a marital relationship under pressure, which may then contribute to a sense of loss and hopelessness that is common amongst many prisoner suicides. As such, marriage per se may not necessarily be a protective factor and it may be the nature of the relationship that is of greater importance (Felthous, 2011).

Situational risk factors

Custodial status

One of the most commonly reported situational variables associated with suicide in prisoners is custodial status, that is whether the prisoner was detained on remand/unconvicted or has already been sentenced/convicted. Previous studies in the UK and Australia have shown around a half of prison suicides were completed by prisoners detained on remand with remand prisoners significantly over-represented amongst suicides (Bogue & Power, 1995; Dalton, 1999). A mixed picture emerges from the more rigorously designed controlled studies of suicides. A particularly strong risk factor for prisoner suicide in England and Wales was being a remand status prisoner (Humber, Webb, Piper, Appleby, & Shaw, 2013); however, studies in Austrian and US prisons failed to show remand status as associated with increased risk (Fruehwald et al., 2004; Winter, 2003). The possible increased risk associated with remand prisoners may be explained, in part, by the sudden immersion into custody and the uncertainty of court outcomes. Another factor that will have influence over the amount of stress experienced by the remand prisoner is that of 'prison type'. Towl & Crighton (2002) suggested the type of prison establishment may be an important risk factor for suicide, with the majority of deaths in England and Wales prisons occurring in local/remand prisons. Therefore, the increased risk of suicide observed in remand prisoners could be as a result of being immersed in an already high-risk environment.

Time in custody

In the UK, approximately a half of prison suicides occur during the first month of custody, with about a tenth of suicides occurring within 24 hours of reception into prison (Shaw et al., 2004). Elsewhere in Europe, the initial period of imprisonment appears to be less of a risky period, with around a quarter of suicides occurring during the first month of custody

(Dalton, 1999; Joukamaa, 1997; Taterelli, Mancinelli, Taggi, & Polidori, 1999). Figures from previous studies of US jail suicides are dramatically higher, where over 80% of suicides occur within a month of reception, with half within 24 hours (Hayes & Rowan, 1988); however, this difference may reflect the higher proportion of remand prisoners held in US jails compared with most European prisons.

It is important to highlight the potential relationship between time into custody and the presence of drug or alcohol use problems. Shaw et al. (2004) reported 59% of suicides in drug-dependent prisoners occurred within seven days of reception into prison, compared with 32% in all suicides. These results suggest that the first few hours of custody are especially traumatic for alcohol and drug abusing prisoners, underlining the importance of timely detoxification facilities for such prisoners.

Arrival into the reception of a prison is likely to be a high-risk moment for many individuals with distress arising because of a problematic past, limited control over the future and the fear of the unknown (World Health Organization, 2007). The person may be ashamed of the fact he or she has been incarcerated, which may lead to a loss of status. Furthermore, the prisoner is put into a group of people he has not selected himself and also made dependent upon prison staff for fulfilling basic human needs. There is a threat of loss of identity in an extremely stressful situation.

Length of sentence

It could be intuitively argued that prisoners facing longer prison terms or indeterminate sentences would be expected to be at a greater risk of suicide than those with shorter sentences, and empirical findings appear to support this view. Topp (1979) reported 66 out of 117 (56%) male sentenced prisoner suicides were serving sentences of 18 months or longer and concluded that a sentence of more than 18 months may increase the propensity to suicide by a factor of 6 or 7. Dooley (1990) reported 84% of prison suicides were serving sentences of greater than 18 months or life sentences, and prisoners serving sentences of 4 years or more were significantly over-represented amongst prison suicides. Suicide rates per 100,000 prisoners have been reported to be 40 for those serving less than 18 months, 75 for prisoners serving more than 5 years and 178 when serving life sentences (Towl & Crighton, 1998). The relationship between longer terms of imprisonment and increased suicide risk may be confounded by the association between more serious crimes and longer sentences, and it can be difficult to separate out the effects of length of sentence with the type of offences the prisoner was sentenced for.

Type of offence

Many reviews of the literature of suicide by prisoners have led to the conclusion that prisoners who commit violent crimes are more likely to complete suicide than non-violent criminals (Lloyd, 1990). In the UK, approximately a quarter of prisoner suicides have been charged with or convicted of a violent or sexual offence (Shaw et al., 2004; Topp, 1979). Across a number of controlled studies, prisoner suicides have been found to be significantly more likely to have been charged or convicted with a violent offence, such as murder or manslaughter (Bogue & Power, 1995; Fazel et al., 2008; Kerkhof & Bernasco, 1990; Winter, 2003). Highly violent offences are associated with a two- to fourfold increase in suicide risk, relative to controls (Fruehwald et al., 2004; Humber et al., 2013). As mentioned previously, the positive relationship between violent offences and suicide risk may be confounded by the longer sentence lengths often attracted by violent offences. Hence it is difficult to be sure if it is the violent offence and its possible association with inwardly directed aggression (Freud, 1957), or the narrowing of future perspectives in the prospect of a long sentence that is the more influential in terms of suicidal behaviour. Nevertheless, it does appear that violent offenders are generally over-represented amongst suicide groups compared with general prison populations.

Clinical risk factors

Previous suicidal behaviour

A history of previous suicidal behaviour is considered to be one of the most important and clinically relevant determinants of suicide risk, associated with a greater than thirtyfold increase in risk of completed suicide in the general population (Cooper et al., 2005; Harris & Barraclough, 1997). Previous suicide attempts are not uncommon amongst suicide victims, although such a history can often be absent especially amongst male suicides where fatal first attempts are significantly more likely than for females (Isometsa & Lonnqvist, 1998). Because much of the research in this area has been conducted within community samples, it is important to consider how the importance of previous suicidal behaviour as a risk factor translates to prisoner populations. Of importance also is the lasting effects of an episode of suicidal behaviour upon the prisoner's ongoing risk of completed suicide, because the likelihood of a completed suicide in the community can be over 100 times greater during the year following a self-harm event (Owens, Horrocks, & House, 2002), with the suicide risk persisting for several years (Jenkins, Hale, Papanastassiou, Crawford, & Tyrer, 2002; Suominen et al., 2004).

A misperception held by some prison staff is that self-harm, self-injury and other non-fatal suicidal behaviours are merely attempts by the prisoner to manipulate their environment in order to meet their needs. Whilst this may be true of some prisoners, the research evidence suggests this to be inaccurate for the majority. For example Dear, Thomson, and Hills (2000) interviewed 74 Australian prisoners within three days of a recent self-harm episode, and just a quarter of those interviewed admitted to having manipulative motives. Only 6 (8%) prisoners reported manipulative motives in the absence of suicidal intent and with low lethality of recent self-harming. These results highlight the potential danger of assuming prisoner self-harm is a manipulative or attention-seeking tactic rather than an act indicative of severe distress and increased risk of suicide.

Investigations of suicide in UK prisons have described a high prevalence of previous self-injury and suicidal behaviour amongst prisoner suicides. Dooley (1990) identified 126 (43%) out of 296 suicides had a recorded history of self-injury, and 65 (22%) had injured themselves during the current incarceration. More recently, Shaw et al. (2004) reported a history of self-harm was present for approximately half of 157 self-inflicted deaths in prisons in England and Wales, although the level of suicidal intent associated with the self-harm events was not determined. In the US, Daniel and Fleming (2006) reported 24 of 37 (65%) suicides in Missouri state prisons had a history of prior suicide attempts, with 18 (49%) having made an attempt prior to incarceration, and 17 (46%) during their current term of imprisonment. Similarly, in a review of completed suicide in California state prisons, 62% of 154 prisoner suicides had a history of suicidal behaviour or statements (Patterson & Hughes, 2008). He, Felthous, and Holzer (2001) found three quarters of suicides in Texan prisons had a prior history of suicide attempts, with over half making multiple attempts during imprisonment. These figures appear to be an increase upon those in reviews of psychological autopsy studies of prisoner suicide in the US published approximately 10 years earlier, where approximately 45% of inmate suicides were known to have previously made 'suicide attempts or gestures' (Hayes, 1995; Schimmel, Sullivan, & Mrad, 1989; White, Schimmel, & Frickey, 2002).

In a case-control study of suicide in Austrian prisons, Fruehwald et al. (2004) reported 108 out of 220 (49%) cases were known to have previously attempted suicide compared with 44 out of 374 (12%) controls. Previous suicide attempts were found to be a significant predictor of completed suicide risk for pre-trial prisoners, associated with an eighteenfold increase in risk, although an attempt history was not found to significantly contribute within the analysis for sentenced prisoners. Similarly, reporting on a controlled study of suicide in Dutch prisons, Blaauw, Kerkhof, and Hayes (2005) found a significantly greater proportion of prior suicidal behaviour amongst completed suicides, with 54 out of 87 (62%) suicides previously attempting suicide compared with 29 out of 245 (12%) randomly selected controls. Finally, in Winter's (2003) case-control study of suicides in US county jails, of the 41 suicides, for which information was available, 20 (49%) had previously attempted suicide – a significantly greater proportion ($p < 0.001$) than the 13% (12 out of 93) for controls.

In summary, a relatively consistent pattern of results has emerged from the range of studies of prisoner suicide investigating the importance of previous suicidal behaviour. Almost two-thirds of completed suicides in prison attempted suicide previously, with up to half making their most recent attempt inside prison. Whilst a history of suicide attempts or self-harm may be present in approximately a tenth of the prisoner population, the level of suicidal behaviour amongst prison suicides is significantly greater and associated with a substantial increase in risk of eventual death. As in community samples, the presence of a history of suicidal behaviour, especially if an attempt occurs within a prison setting, should alert staff to the exceptional level of risk presented by the prisoner. The endurance of such a risk has not been examined for prison suicides with no long-term follow-up studies of prisoners following an episode of self-harm or self-injurious behaviour. And so it remains unknown how far into an individual's clinical history we should look to ascertain the most accurate impression of his or her current risk.

Psychiatric diagnoses and contact with mental health care services

> There has been an acceptance for some time that mental disorder is a major contributor to suicide in the general population, it has in contrast been suggested that much of the suicidal behaviour in prisons is socially determined and unrelated to the presence of defined mental disorder.
>
> (Jenkins et al., 2005, p. 258)

One of the main risk factors for suicide in the community is the presence of mental health problems, with as many as 9 out of 10 suicides having a psychiatric history (Harris & Barraclough, 1997), but what role do mental health problems play amongst prisoner suicides? One of the first UK studies to report on the incidence of a psychiatric history amongst prison suicides was by Topp (1979) who identified 70 out of 186 (38%) prison suicides had had psychiatric treatment in the past, of which 56 (30%) were in-patient admissions. Furthermore, 69% of prison suicides had seen a doctor concerning a psychiatric complaint whilst in custody for which 39% were prescribed treatment. Definite or probable depressive episodes were reported for 98 (52%) prisoners. In a systematic study of prison suicide in England and Wales, Dooley (1990) reported that almost a third of cases had had previous contact with psychiatric services, with a quarter admitted as in-patients. Regarding treatment, 67 (23%) prisoners had received psychiatric medication in the month prior to their suicide. Of the 97 cases with a history of psychiatric contact, 21 (22%) had a primary diagnosis of psychoses and 22 (23%) had a depressive illness. Another study of prison suicide in England and Wales described the clinical characteristics of 157 self-inflicted deaths (Shaw et al., 2004). Again, almost a third (46) of prison suicides had previously been in contact with psychiatric services and 19 (12%) had been in-patients. A total of 110 prisoners (70%) had at least one psychiatric diagnosis, with an affective disorder the primary diagnosis for 26 (17%) prisoners and schizophrenia for 10 (6%) prisoners, and 46 (29%) prison suicides had more than one psychiatric diagnosis. At the time of death, 26 (17%) suicides were prison hospital in-patients and 50 (32%) had been referred to a psychiatrist since being imprisoned.

In Scottish prisons, Backett (1987) reported 20 of 33 (62%) suicides had a history of psychiatric contact and 11 (33%) had received in-patient treatment prior to imprisonment. Two (18%) prisoners had a depressive disorder, and 2 (18%) had schizophrenia. In a later study of suicide in Scottish prisons, Bogue and Power (1995) identified a history of in-patient psychiatric treatment for 14 (17%) out of 88 suicides with 20 (24%) prisoners seeing a psychiatrist whilst in custody, prior to their death. Eleven (13%) cases had a diagnosis of a depressive illness and 4 (5%) had a psychotic illness.

In Tatarelli et al.'s (1999) study of suicide in Italian prisons, 73% of prisoner suicides had a diagnosable mental disorder, most commonly depression in 62% of cases. Joukamaa (1997) reported 73% of suicides in Finnish prisons had previously received care from a doctor or nurse for mental health problems at some time during their confinement, with over half (51%) during the week prior to death. He et al. (2001) found 19 out of 25 (76%) suicides in Texan prisons could be identified as having mental health problems, with the most common diagnoses being mood disorders (64%), psychoses (44%) and anxiety disorders (28%). He et al. (2001) also reported that 88% of suicide victims had had two or more psychiatric diagnoses made during incarceration, when Axis I and II diagnoses were combined. In a study of suicide in New York State correctional facilities, Kovasznay, Miraglia, Beer, and Way (2004) identified 76 inmate suicides of which 64 (84%) received mental health services at some point during their last incarceration. Finally, Green, Kendall, Andre, Looman, and Polvi (1993) reported on 133 suicides in Canadian prisons and found 59 (44%) had at least one prior prison psychiatric admission, 43 (32%) had been hospitalised outside of prison and 39 (29%) had received psychiatric treatment as an out-patient.

A common criticism of these descriptive studies investigating the link between prison suicide and mental health problems is the absence of a representative control group, which would allow comparisons to be made with the general prisoner population. This issue has been addressed in relatively few controlled studies of prisoner suicide. For instance Kerkhof and Bernasco (1990) reported on 44 completed and 198 attempted suicides by jail and prison inmates in the Netherlands, with control groups randomly selected from the general inmate populations for the two suicide groups. Over half (56%) of completed suicides were prescribed psychotropic medication compared with 27% of controls ($p < 0.001$), similarly amongst attempted suicides, 59% were prescribed medication compared with 31% of controls ($p < 0.001$). More recently, Blaauw et al. (2005) identified suicides in Dutch prisons were significantly more likely to have had a 'history of psychiatric care' than for the general prison population ($p < 0.001$), with such a history associated with an elevenfold increase in suicide risk, even when allowing for the contribution of other key demographic and situational predictors of suicide risk. Fruehwald et al. (2004) reported 81 out of 139 (58%) suicides in Austrian prisons were receiving psychiatric medication compared with 44 out of 329 (13%) controls, with 67% of cases, versus 10% of controls, attracting a psychiatric diagnosis. Regression analyses of pre-trial prisoners identified being on psychiatric medication as one of the major risk factors for suicide associated with a twenty-six-fold increase in risk ($OR = 26.9$, 95% CI 3.2–223.5, $p = 0.0023$), although it's likely that the *need* to be on such medication is the true risk factor. In a similar analysis for sentenced prisoners, having a psychiatric diagnosis was a major risk factor ($OR = 17.4$, 95% CI 4.2–71.7, $p < 0.0001$). In a study of suicide in US jails by Goss, Peterson, Smith, Kalb, and Brodey (2002), a review of each suicide attempter's inmate medical record and officers' logs revealed inmates who attempted suicide were significantly more likely to have a chronic psychiatric problem than the general inmate population (77% vs. 15%, $p < 0.01$). Furthermore, Winter (2003) collected data on suicides in US county jails and a comparison sample from a random selection of the general jail population. Of the 58 suicides for which psychiatric history was made available, 17 (29%) had previously indicated mental health problems compared with 17 out of 104 (16%) controls. In a recent case-control study of risk factors for prisoner suicide in England and Wales, Humber et al. (2013) highlighted particularly strong associations between prisoner suicide and previous contact with mental health services, especially previous psychiatric inpatient admission, having received a psychiatric diagnosis and being in the receipt of psychotropic medication at reception into prison, with such risk factors associated with a three- to sixfold increase in the likelihood of completed suicide.

In summary, a number of studies have investigated the relationship between prison suicide and mental health problems, but with mixed results. Of those prisoners that completed suicide, descriptive studies have suggested between 20% and 80% had been in contact with mental health-care services either prior to or during their custody. Psychiatric diagnoses were common among prison suicides, with depressive disorders (20–30%) and psychotic disorders (5–20%) common primary diagnoses, although as many as 80–90% of suicides received multiple diagnoses. Controlled studies of prisoner suicide have shown a much clearer association between mental health problems and an increased risk of suicide. Methodological problems beset this research topic, though. First, the high prevalence of mental health problems and need for mental health services by prisoner suicides seems to match that found amongst the general prisoner population, thus undermining the role of mental health problems as a specific risk factor for prison suicide. And second, studies conducted to examine this risk factor have varied considerably in their operationalisation of the term 'mental illness' and how it can be measured, often using 'history of psychiatric contact' in the absence of current psychiatric diagnoses. Such a proxy measure is often unreliable and provides little meaningful insight into the mental state of the prisoner immediately prior to the suicide and may also refer to contact relating to a psychiatric problem from many years previously. Furthermore, a history of psychiatric contact is dependent on the help-seeking behaviour of the prisoner and the quality of the services provided by the prison and community health services. Consequently, a prisoner with no previous contact with mental healthcare services should not be assumed to have no mental health problems or ongoing psychological distress at the time of a suicidal death. Prisoners tend to come from disenfranchised groups within society, with a reluctance to engage with statutory services (Social Exclusion Unit, 2002).

Substance use

Drug and alcohol misuse can affect a prisoner's risk of suicide in a number of different ways. First, from epidemiological studies, a history of substance misuse is known to elevate an individual's risk of suicide (Harris & Barraclough, 1997). Second, during his or her first few weeks into custody, a prisoner's propensity to attempt suicide may be influenced if he or she is also suffering from withdrawal of drugs or alcohol, or both (Towl & Crighton, 1998). And third, the actual consumption of alcohol, drugs or both can increase a person's immediate likelihood for suicidal behaviour, since one effect of substances is the disinhibition of behaviour (Hayes, 1983).

A range of studies has reported on the prevalence of substance use amongst prison suicides; however, information on control groups or, at least, the general prison population at the time of these studies was often not provided, hence informative comparisons were not possible. In England and Wales, Topp (1979) identified 55 out of 186 (30%) prisoner suicides had had an alcohol problem and 21 (22%) a drug problem, and Dooley (1990) reported 85 out of 295 (29%) prisoner suicides had a history of alcohol abuse and 69 (23%) of drug abuse. In Shaw et al.'s (2004) descriptive study of suicide by prisoners, the most common primary diagnosis was drug dependence in 39 out of 157 (27%) cases for which clinical information was obtained. Backett (1987) reported that 15 out of 33 (45%) suicides in Scottish prisons were documented as having had an alcohol- or drug-related problem. Bogue and Power (1995) identified 23 out of 79 (29%) Scottish prison suicides had a history of alcohol abuse, 15 (19%) drug abuse and a further 6 (8%) had both. In their study of suicide in Italian prisons, Tatarelli et al. (1999) found 58 out of 100 suicides had previously been identified as 'drug addicts'. Kerkhof and Bernasco (1990) interviewed 25 inmates in Dutch jails and prisons who had recently attempted suicide. They found that 17 (68%) were seriously addicted to alcohol, drugs or both. The addiction was stated by inmate interviewees to be a clear and contributing factor in the aetiology of their attempt.

The link between substance misuse and suicide has also been examined in US jails and prisons. Hayes and Rowan (1988) identified 132 out of 219 (60%) suicides as under the influence of alcohol, drugs or both at the time of death. He et al. (2001) reported that 17 out of 25 (68%) suicides in Texan prisons had a history of alcohol abuse or dependence, 68% had drug abuse or dependence and 48% had both alcohol and drug abuse or dependence histories.

The inclusion of a control group of non-suicidal prisoners enables an informed consideration of substance use as a potential risk factor for prison suicide. Goss et al. (2002) found that the proportion of suicide attempters in Washington state jails with a history of substance misuse (64%) was similar to that for inmates in the general jail population (60%). However, in an analysis of suicide attempts in a Midwestern state's jails, Winter (2003) found that suicide attempters were significantly more likely to have a history of drug or alcohol abuse, prior to custody, than controls (chi^2 = 16.598, df = 3, p < 0.001). In their case-control study of suicide in Austrian prisons, Fruehwald et al. (2004) also found substance misuse to be significantly more likely among suicide cases than controls (p < 0.01).

The contribution of substance use and withdrawal problems upon the prisoner's suicidal death has also been investigated within a few, albeit small-scale, studies. For example of the 15 suicides in Scottish prisons documented to have had alcohol- or drug-related problems, 9 (60%) took place within the first week of custody (Backett, 1987). Similarly, Bogue and Power (1995) identified 18 out of 27 (67%) prisoners that completed suicide during their first week of entering custody were dependent upon drugs, alcohol or both. These two Scottish studies provide some support for the link between suicide and substance withdrawal. Hayes and Rowan (1988) reported an overwhelming majority (82%) of suicide victims in US holding facilities (0–48 hours) were intoxicated compared with 49% of victims in detention facilities (over 48 hours), highlighting the disinhibition effects of such substances. Davis and Muscat (1993) obtained data on the length of incarceration for 174 cases of jail suicide of which 102 suicides (59%) occurred within the first 24 hours. Even after controlling for the time of reception, cases with alcohol-related offences were significantly more likely to complete suicide within the first 24 hours than were other cases (adj. RR = 6.9, 95% CI 3.1–15.4, p < 0.05). Furthermore, among all cases completing suicide in the first 24 hours, those cases intoxicated at the time of reception killed themselves significantly more rapidly (9.0±1.6 hours) compared with other cases (16.8±1.3 hours).

In summary, it is well known that substance misuse is common in prisoner populations, making it difficult for such a factor to be used as a reliable indicator for suicide risk. Nevertheless, the proportion of prison suicides with a history or diagnosis of alcohol or drug abuse or dependence (30–70%) generally seems to be higher when compared with non-suicidal control groups or the prison populations from which the suicide samples were originally drawn. Additionally, the reception of offenders with pre-existing substance use problems into jails or prisons should be considered as a period of high risk.

Personality disorder

Results from psychiatric morbidity surveys of prisoners suggest a high prevalence of personality disorder amongst prisoner populations with 64–78% of male prisoners and 42–50% of female prisoners diagnosed with a personality disorder (Fazel & Danesh, 2002; Singleton, Meltzer, Gatword, Coid, & Deasy, 1998). Studies of personality disorder and suicide in the community have shown suicide to be seven times more likely amongst those with a personality disorder (Harris & Barraclough, 1997). However, a high baseline prevalence of personality disorder makes it difficult for such a psychiatric diagnosis to be a significant discriminator for suicide in prisoners.

In England and Wales, Dooley (1990) reported that 25 out of 97 (26%) prison suicides that had a psychiatric history also had a primary diagnosis of a personality disorder, and Shaw et al. (2004) identified 15 (10%) suicides had a primary diagnosis of a personality disorder. In Scotland, Backett (1987) identified 4 out of 11 (36%) male suicides had a personality disorder, although Bogue and Power (1995) found only 4 out of 79 (5%) prison suicides had a personality disorder, although it was pointed out that such information was not routinely recorded in a prisoner's central record. Tatarelli et al. (1999) reported 8–10% of suicides in Italian prisons had a personality disorder. In the US, He et al. (2001) reported that personality disorders were recorded in only 4% of inmates at reception into custody; however, 56% of inmates were later diagnosed during their incarceration. All diagnoses were for Borderline or Anti-social personality disorder. And so it appears that the proportion of prison suicides that had previously been diagnosed with a personality disorder may be some way below the figure previously reported in the psychiatric morbidity surveys, although most of these studies report only primary diagnoses. It may be that a diagnosis of a personality disorder for a prisoner is more likely to be seen as a secondary diagnosis if the prisoner had a comorbid Axis I diagnosis. Such 'prioritising' of diagnoses would lead to a misleadingly low prevalence of personality disorder amongst prisoner suicides.

Another approach to the relationship between personality disorder and prison suicide was adopted by Verona, Patrick, and Joiner (2001), who assessed 313 male prison inmates in a Florida prison using the Psychopathy Checklist – Revised (PCL-R; Hare, 1991) and *Diagnostic and Statistical Manual For Mental Disorders* diagnostic criteria (American Psychiatric Association, 1994) for Anti-social Personality Disorder. Twenty-four (8%) prisoners were assessed as having previously attempted suicide according to self-reports in structured interviews or from information contained in prison records. A significant positive relationship was found between PCL-R scores and previous suicide attempts ($r = 0.11$, $p < 0.05$). By conducting a logistic regression analysis, the authors were able to assess the unique contributions of the two PCL-R factors. This analysis found that factor 2 (chronic anti-social deviance) contributed significantly ($OR = 2.12$, $p < 0.01$) but factor 1 (affective and interpersonal features) did not ($OR = 0.77$, $p = 0.33$).

In conclusion, a number of descriptive studies have reported on the possible relationship between prison suicide and personality disorder. Unfortunately, variation in the design and sampling strategies of these studies has led to a wide range of proportions, with personality disorder present in 5–30% of prison suicides. In the absence of any large-scale controlled study of personality disorder amongst completed prisoner suicides, the level of risk associated with such a diagnosis remains largely unknown.

References

American Psychiatric Association. (1994). *Diagnostic and statistical manual for mental disorders* (4th ed.). Washington, DC: Author.

Backett, S.A. (1987). Suicide in Scottish prisons. *British Journal of Psychiatry, 151*, 218–221.

Blaauw, E., Kerkhof, J.F.M., & Hayes, L.M. (2005). Demographic, criminal and psychiatric factors related to inmate suicide. *Suicide and Life Threatening Behavior, 35*(1), 63–75.

Bogue, J., & Power, K. (1995). Suicide in Scottish Prisons, 1976–1993. *Journal of Forensic Psyciatry, 6*(3), pp. 527–540.

Cooper, J., Kapur, N., Webb, R., Lawlor, M., Guthrie, E., Mackway-Jones, K., & Appleby, L. (2005). Suicide after deliberate self-harm: A 4 year cohort study. *American Journal of Psychiatry, 162*, 297–303.

Dalton, V. (1999). Suicide in prison, 1980 to 1998: A national overview. *Trends & Issues in Crime and Criminal Justice, no. 126*. Canberra, ACT: Australian Institute of Criminology.

Daniel, A.E., & Fleming, J. (2006). Suicides in a state correctional system, 1992–2002: A review. *Journal of Correctional Health Care, 12*(1), 24–35.

Davis, M.S., & Muscat, J.E. (1993). An epidemiologic study of alcohol and suicide risk in Ohio jails and lockups, 1975–1984. *Journal of Criminal Justice, 21*, 277–283.

Dear, G.E., Thomson, D.M., and Hills, A.M. (2000). Self-harm in prison: Manipulators can also be suicide attempters. *Criminal Justice and Behavior, 27*(2), 160–175.

Dooley, E. (1990). Prison suicide in England and Wales, 1972–87. *British Journal of Psychiatry, 156*, 40–45.

Fazel, S., Cartwright, J., Norman-Nott, A., & Hawton, K. (2008). Suicide in prisoners: A systematic review of risk factors. *Journal of Clinical Psychiatry, 69*(11), 1721–1731.

Fazel, S., & Danesh, J. (2002). Serious mental disorder in 23,000 prisoners: A systematic review of 62 surveys. *Lancet, 359,* 545–550.

Felthous, A.R. (2011). Suicide behind bars: Trends, inconsistencies, and practical implications. *Journal of Forensic Sciences, 56*(6), 1541–1555.

Freud, S. (1957). Mourning and melancholia. In J. Strachey (Ed. & Trans.) *The standard edition of the complete psychological works of Sigmund Freud* (Vol. 14, pp. 237–260). London, UK: Hogarth Press. (Original work published 1917)

Fruehwald, S., Frottier, P., Matschnig, T., König, F., & Bauer, P. (2004). Suicide in custody: a case-control study, *British Journal of Psychiatry, 185,* 494–498.

Goss, J.R., Peterson, K., Smith, L.W., Kalb, K., & Brodey, B.B. (2002). Characteristics of suicide attempts in a large urban jail system with an established suicide prevention program. *Psychiatric Services, 53*(5), 574–579.

Green, C., Kendall, K., Andre, G., Looman, T., & Polvi, N. (1993). A study of 133 suicides among Canadian federal prisoners. *Medicine, Science and the Law, 33*(2), 121–127.

Hare, R.D. (1991). *The Hare Psychopathy Checklist – Revised.* Toronto, ON, Canada: Multi-Health Systems.

Harris, E.C., & Barraclough, B. (1997). Suicide as an outcome for mental disorders: A meta-analysis. *British Journal of Psychiatry, 170,* 205–228.

Hayes, L.M. (1983). And darkness closes in . . . a national study of jail suicides. *Criminal Justice and Behaviour, 10*(4), 461–484.

Hayes, L.M. (1995). *Prison suicide: An overview and guide to prevention.* Washington, DC: US Department of Justice, National Institute of Corrections.

Hayes, L.M., & Rowan, J.R. (1988). *National study of jail suicides: Seven years later.* Alexandria, VA: National Center on Institutions and Alternatives. Sponsored by National Institute of Corrections, US Department of Justice.

He, X-Y., Felthous, A.R., Holzer, C.E., & Nathan, P. (2001). Factors in prison suicide: One year study in Texas. *Journal of Forensic Sciences, 46*(4), 896–901.

Humber, N., Webb, R., Piper, M., Appleby, L., & Shaw, J. (2013). A national case-control study of risk factors among prisoners in England and Wales. *Social Psychiatry and Psychiatric Epidemiology, 48,* 1177–1185.

Isometsa, E.T., & Lonnqvist, J.K. (1998). Suicide attempts preceding completed suicide. *British Journal of Psychiatry, 173,* 531–535.

Jenkins, G.R., Hale, R., Papanastassiou, M., Crawford, M.J., & Tyrer, P. (2002). Suicide rate 22 years after parasuicide cohort study. *British Medical Journal, 325,* 1155.

Jenkins, R., Bhugra, D., Meltzer, H., Singleton, N., Bebbington, P., Brugha, T., . . . Paton, J. (2005). Psychiatric and social aspects of suicidal behaviour in prisons. *Psychological Medicine, 35,* 257–269.

Joukamaa, M. (1997). Prison suicide in Finland, 1969–1992. *Forensic Science International, 89,* 167–174.

Kerkhof, J.F.M., & Bernasco, W. (1990). Suicidal behaviour in jails and prisons in the Netherlands: Incidence, characteristics, and prevention. *Suicide and Life-Threatening Behavior, 20*(2), 123–137.

Kovasznay, B., Miraglia, R., Beer, R., & Way, B. (2004). Reducing suicide in New York State correctional facilities. *Psychiatric Quarterly, 75*(1), 61–70.

Lloyd, C. (1990). *Suicide and self-injury in prison: A literature review*. London, UK: Home Office.

Owens, D., Horrocks, J., & House, A. (2002). Fatal and non-fatal repetition of self-harm. *British Journal of Psychiatry, 181*, 193–199.

Patterson, R. F., & Hughes, K. (2008). Review of completed suicides in the California Department of Corrections and Rehabilitation, 1999 to 2004. *Psychiatric Services, 59*, 676–682.

Schimmel, D., Sullivan, J., & Mrad, D. (1989). Suicide prevention: Is it working in the federal prison system? *Federal Prisons Journal, 1*(1), 20–24.

Shaw, J., Baker, D., Hunt, I. M., Moloney, A., & Appleby, L. (2004). Suicide by prisoners: A national clinical survey. *British Journal of Psychiatry, 184*, 263–267.

Singleton, N., Meltzer, H., Gatword, R., Coid, J., & Deasy, D. (1998). *Psychiatric morbidity among prisoners in England and Wales*. London, UK: Home Office.

Social Exclusion Unit. (2002). *Reducing re-offending by ex-prisoners*. London, UK: Author.

Suominen, K., Isometsa, E. T., Suokas, J., Haukka, J., Achte, K., & Lonnqvist, J. K. (2004). Completed suicide after a suicide attempt: A 37 year follow-up study. *American Journal of Psychiatry, 161*(3), 563–564.

Tatarelli, R., Mancinelli, I., Taggi, F., & Polidori, G. (1999). Suicide in Italian prisons in 1996 and 1997: A descriptive epidemiological study. *International Journal of Offender Therapy and Comparative Criminology, 43*(4), 438–447.

Topp, D. O. (1979). Suicide in prison. *British Journal of Psychiatry, 134*, 24–27.

Towl, G. J., & Crighton, D. A. (1998). Suicide in prisons in England and Wales from 1988 to 1995. *Criminal Behaviour and Mental Health, 8*, 184–192.

Towl, G. J., & Crighton, D. A. (2002). Risk assessment and management. In G. J. Towl, L. Snow, & M. McHugh (Eds.), *Suicide in prisons* (pp. 66–92). Oxford, UK: BPS Blackwell.

Verona, E., Patrick, C. J., & Joiner, T. E. (2001). Psychopathy, antisocial personality, and suicide risk. *Journal of Abnormal Psychology, 110*(3), 462–470.

Way, B. B., Miraglia, R., Sawyer, D. A., Beer, R., & Eddy, J. (2005). Factors related to suicide in New York state prisons. *International Journal of Law and Psychiatry, 28*, 207–221.

White, T. W., Schimmel, D. J., & Frickey, R. (2002). A comprehensive analysis of suicide in federal prisons: A fifteen-year review. *Journal of Correctional Health Care, 9*(3), 321–343.

Winter, M. M. (2003). County jail suicides in a Midwestern state: Moving beyond the use of profiles. *The Prison Journal, 83*(2), 130–148.

World Health Organization. (2007). *Health in prisons: A WHO guide to the essentials in prison health*. Geneva, Switzerland: Author.

3 Psychological models of suicidal ideation and behaviour

Patricia Gooding and Daniel Pratt

Why are psychological models of suicide needed?

There are four reasons why a theoretical approach is essential to understanding the ways in which suicidal thoughts and feelings are triggered and maintained. As we have seen in the previous chapter, one approach to suicide prevention is based on identifying epidemiological risk factors that are associated with suicide attempts and completions (Brown, Beck, Steer, & Grisham, 2000; Fawcett, Busch, Jacobs, Kravitz, & Fogg, 1997; Gunnel, Harbord, Singleton, Jenkins, & Lewis, 2004). Within the general population, these risk factors include being unemployed, homeless, male and divorced (Hawton & van Heeringen, 2009). One of the main limitations of this approach and a key reason why a psychological model of suicide is needed is that the risk-based approach to understanding suicide, although useful in indicating in what strata of society problems lie, is not specific enough (Tarrier et al., 2013). People may be identified as being at risk of suicide on the basis of these epidemiological risk factors, when in fact they are not thinking of, or planning, suicide. In other words, an epidemiological risk-based approach may produce too many false positives to be practically useful at an individual level. Consequently, assessment procedures based only on risk factors will be ineffective and inefficient. Conversely, false negatives (i.e. identifying an individual as not suicidal when he or she is at risk) represents a dangerous possibility with potentially serious consequences (Granello, 2010).

A second reason why we need psychological models of suicide is that an epidemiological risk-based approach can often identify factors that are hard to change. For example going through a divorce and having financial difficulties are difficult to change, and especially difficult to change quickly. This has the knock-on effect that intervention and treatment efforts cannot be used to effectively change epidemiological risk factors. An alternative approach could be to identify the psychological processes and mechanisms underlying suicide that are potentially changeable within an intervention. For example people who are suicidal often say that the psychological pain that they are suffering is too great to cope with, and that they need to escape from that psychological pain (Shneidman, 1993). From a therapeutic perspective, it may be possible to work with someone who is suicidal to identify other forms of escape besides suicide. For example a person whose suicidal ideation is triggered when perceiving rejection and abandonment from loved ones may derive benefit from improved interpersonal problem \-solving skills. Within a psychological intervention, the therapist and client may also endeavor to find ways of reducing psychological pain, or learning to accept or tolerate that pain, whilst focusing on what is of value to the client (Tarrier et al., 2013).

The third reason that we need psychological models of suicide is that to be able to facilitate behaviour change, we need to know the psychological processes and mechanisms that underlie the unwanted behaviour, which in this case is experiencing suicidal thoughts, feelings and behaviours. Once these psychological processes that underlie suicidality have been identified, the next objective is to better understand how they interact or work together to trigger and maintain suicidal thoughts and behaviours. Such an informed understanding would then feed into the focus of the psychological intervention.

The fourth reason for developing theoretical models is that the psychological mechanisms being postulated can be tested. Without a test of the model, it remains mere speculation whether the model accurately describes the mechanisms underlying suicidality. The model should develop, be amended and be tested iteratively, leading to greater refinement of the model and to a better, more in-depth understanding of the psychological processes, and interactions between those processes, that trigger and maintain suicidal thoughts and behaviours. Once we have a sophisticated, empirically tested model of the psychological processes that lead to suicidality, then we can be more confident that we have an evidence base on which to develop effective psychological interventions to ameliorate suicidal thoughts and behaviours (Tarrier et al., 2013; Tarrier et al., 2014).

Contrasting diagnostic and psychological models of suicide

Experiencing suicidal thoughts, plans and behaviours is common in those diagnosed with a number of serious psychiatric illnesses, such as schizophrenia, post-traumatic stress disorder (PTSD), major unipolar depression and bipolar disorder (Hawton, Comabella, Haw, & Saunders, 2013; Hawton & van Heeringen, 2009). A medical diagnostic approach to understanding suicidality focuses primarily upon the psychiatric illness that an individual is diagnosed with, and often views suicidality as arising from the specific symptoms of the illness or, in the case of a depressive episode, even as a symptom itself. The rationale can then be applied that if the psychiatric illness can be successfully treated then the person's levels of suicidality will correspondingly reduce, because suicidal thoughts and behaviours are understood as an off-shoot of the mental illness. If this were true, then a psychological model of suicidality would, quite simply, not be necessary.

Our psychological argument is that suicide should be understood independently of a psychiatric diagnosis that a person has been given (Tarrier et al., 2013). However, this is not to say any psychiatric disorder experienced by the individual should not attract the required medical treatment, if required. Several points are presented to support this claim.

First, psychiatric diagnoses are often co-morbid (Kessler, Chiu, Demler, Merikangas, & Walters, 2005). For example PTSD often co-occurs with major depression (Panagioti, Gooding, & Tarrier, 2012), and major depression is often accompanied by anxiety (Kessler et al., 2011). With such a high prevalence of co-morbid psychiatric disorders, the question arises as to whether it is necessary to elicit improvements in the symptoms of all co-morbid disorders to alleviate suicidality. If the answer to that question is no, then there needs to be a rationale as to which diagnoses should be targeted with respect to improving suicidality. At present, we believe there is no such rationale.

Second, at our Understanding the Psychology of Suicide (UPSide) research group at the University of Manchester, we work alongside a number of service users with lived experience of suicidal thoughts and behaviours. They have been given a variety of psychiatric diagnoses. They tell us consistently that reducing symptoms of a psychiatric disorder does not necessarily result in less frequency or severity of suicidal thoughts and behaviours. This is powerful information because it comes from people who have to live with challenging and distressing symptoms of psychiatric disorders day in and day out. The importance of incorporating service user experiences and views within our approach to suicide prevention is further discussed in Chapter 6.

Third, some psychiatric medications can potentially worsen suicidal thoughts and behaviours. For example there has been longstanding controversy surrounding the safety and efficacy of certain anti-depressant medications (e.g. Gunnel, Saperia, & Ashby, 2005; Whittington et al., 2004). Statements from the UK Medicines and Healthcare products Regulatory Agency and the US Food and Drug Administration have contraindicated the use of certain anti-depressants warning that such medications pose a small but significantly increased risk of suicidal ideation. This evidence weakens the argument that the pharmacological treatment of psychiatric symptoms goes hand-in-hand with reductions in suicidality. Suicide prevention efforts require the development of evidence-based treatments and interventions that have been proven to demonstrate improvements in suicidality with minimal, if any, negative side effects. Psychological approaches, especially cognitive behavioural therapies, are now indicated as important treatment components for individuals engaging in suicidal behaviours (National Institute for Health and Care Excellence, 2011).

Finally, our psychological approach to understanding suicidality asks what the evidence is for

1   Transdiagnostic components of suicidality that seem common across a number of psychological difficulties;
2   Diagnostic-specific components of suicidality, such as command hallucinations experienced by some people with a diagnosis on the schizophrenia spectrum that instruct sufferers to kill themselves, and;
3   Interactions between transdiagnostic components and diagnostic-specific components.

In other words, we encourage a logical approach which is based on data rather than on assumptions (Bolton, Gooding, Kapur, Barrowclough, & Tarrier, 2007).

The intention of our UPSide research group has always been to move beyond the restrictions of traditional uni-disciplinary boundaries towards considering suicidality as the result of a multi-factorial interaction of biological, psychological and social factors. As such, a broadened understanding across all of these areas is required for a sufficient explanation of suicide to be offered.

What are the current psychological models that have been developed to explain suicidal thoughts and behaviours?

Four contemporary psychological models of suicide will now be discussed: the Cry of Pain model, the Interpersonal Theory, the Integrated Motivational Volitional model and the Schematic Appraisals Model.

The Cry of Pain model

One of the most influential, contemporary psychological models of suicide is the Cry of Pain model developed by Mark Williams and colleagues

(Williams, 1997). The Cry of Pain model is a bio-psychosocial model and has six identifiable components. The first two describe the presence of stressors, which may be external (e.g. financial debt, divorce) or internal (e.g. command hallucinations), and the perception that these stressors are negative. The third factor relates to a body of evidence linking psychological disorders to negative processing biases (Joormann & D'Avanzato, 2010; Klewchuk, McCusker, Mulholland, & Shannon, 2007; Morrison & O'Connor, 2008; Taylor & John, 2004). For example anxiety disorders have been linked to directing attention to fearful stimuli, people who experience depression judge neutral stimuli as being negative, and reasoning biases are often observed in those with psychosis, for example jumping to conclusions. The fourth factor rests on findings that feelings and perceptions of hopelessness are highly correlated with suicidality, more so than depression (e.g. Young et al., 1996). There are two key characteristics of hopelessness. The first is that perceptions of the future are negative, and the second is more that the future is seen as promising nothing that is positive (MacLeod, Rose, & Williams, 1993; O'Connor & Cassidy, 2007). The fifth factor is that an individual perceives himself or herself to have poor social support, and that there is no possibility of being rescued. The sixth factor is that people who are suicidal need to have a knowledge of the means to kill themselves if they are to enact suicide. It is postulated that all six factors feed into perceptions of defeat and entrapment.

The Interpersonal Theory

Thomas Joiner and colleagues (Joiner, Van Orden, Witte, & Rudd, 2009) proposed the Interpersonal Theory of suicide comprising three components: a feeling of being a burden upon significant others, a perception of thwarted belongingness and habituation to pain (Christensen, Batterham, Soubelet, & Mackinnon, 2013; Selby & Joiner, 2013; Van Orden et al., 2010). Evidence for this model grew from work with suicidal war veterans who were in the situation of experiencing and witnessing extreme physical pain and also dealing with the emotional consequences of existing in a highly threatening war context. The argument is that experiencing physical pain leads to a degree of habituation to that pain, which aids suicide attempts. Further support for this theory has come from diverse populations, including samples with psychiatric diagnoses and community dwelling individuals of differing ages (Joiner, Van Orden, Witte, Selby, et al., 2009; Sachs-Ericsson et al., 2014; Van Orden et al., 2010).

The Integrated Motivational Volitional model

The Integrated Motivational Volitional (IMV) model of suicide attempts to integrate and advance key components of previous suicide models, primarily sharing similarities with Williams's Cry of Pain model and Joiner's Interpersonal Theory (O'Connor & Nock, 2014). The IMV is a socio-cognitive model that aims to understand the pathways to suicidal thoughts and behaviours using a grid-like matrix. A pre-motivational phase comprises various background factors and life events that elevate an individual's predisposition to suicide. The initial stage of the motivational phase occurs when appraisals of acute or chronic stressors focus upon defeat or humiliation, which is then followed by feelings of entrapment, which in turn precedes suicidal ideation and intent. An individual may transition from feeling defeated to trapped or from trapped to suicidal if stage-specific moderators are present, including problem-solving deficits, rumination, burdensomeness and lack of social support. Importantly, the IMV model proposes that individuals move from suicidal ideation to suicidal behaviour only when volitional moderators are present, which include impulsivity, planning and access to means. A potential, although perhaps fundamental, issue with the IMV model relates to the emphasis that is placed upon the motivation for suicide coming from a progression from suicidal thoughts and plans to actual attempts. We argue that preceding 'stages' of completed suicide should not be considered to be linear, because the occurrence of suicidal behaviour may not be entirely determinable from a prior sequence of appraisals of defeat, entrapment, hopelessness and a final intent to act (Tarrier et al., 2013).

The Schematic Appraisals Model of Suicide (SAMS)

The SAMS builds on the foundations laid down by the Cry of Pain model (Bolton et al., 2007; Williams, 1997). The SAMS comprises three components, namely: the operation of information/cognitive processing biases, the development and maintenance of suicide schema and the operation of a negatively biased appraisals system. The first two components advance the literature base underpinning the Cry of Pain model of suicide. The third component represents a novel element that attempted to identify the types of psychological appraisals or evaluations that were important in the pathways to suicidality (Johnson, Gooding, & Tarrier, 2008; Tarrier et al., 2013; Tarrier et al., 2014).

We have amassed a body of evidence which shows that the pathways to suicide are multi-dimensional. In people experiencing psychosis and in people experiencing PTSD, who may also have co-morbid depressive disorders, negative appraisals of social support, social problem solving and emotional regulation led to perceptions of defeat and entrapment (Panagioti, Gooding, Dunn, & Tarrier, 2011; Panagioti, Gooding, Taylor, & Tarrier, 2014; Taylor, Gooding, Wood, & Tarrier, 2011). The perceptions of defeat and entrapment are key in the final steps to experiencing suicidal thoughts and behaviours. Furthermore, our work indicates that although there are trans-diagnostic psychological factors which amplify suicidality, such as negative appraisals, there are also diagnosis specific factors in relation to schizophrenia and PTSD (Panagioti et al., 2014; Taylor, Gooding, Wood, & Tarrier, 2010).

What should theories consider when applied to a prison setting?

One of the major issues to consider when understanding how to apply existing psychological models of suicide to prisoners is the interaction between the individual prisoner and his or her environment, that is the prison setting. The impact of imprisonment varies widely from individual to individual. However, many would agree that incarceration requires considerable adjustment (Dhami, Ayton, & Loewenstein, 2007; Harvey, 2007). Prison is painful, and some individuals struggle to successfully make the necessary adjustments to living that can cause significant distress, deprivation and extremely atypical patterns of interacting with others. The effects of imprisonment are not irreversible, although there is a consensus that prison can produce negative, long-lasting change with stronger effects more likely for harsher prison environments (Bonta & Gendreau, 1990). Although prisons can be difficult and demanding environments to adjust to, the adaptation required of prisoners is a natural and normal process in response to the unnatural and abnormal conditions of prisoner life (Haney, 2003). This adjustment process involves the integration of prison norms into the prisoner's own habits of thinking, feeling and behaving. As such, this process takes time, and the longer an individual has been incarcerated during his or her lifetime, the more significant this 'institutional transformation' tends to be (Johnson & Rhodes, 2008).

Whilst conducting our own investigations into the psychology of prisoner suicide, according to the SAMS model, we have become aware of the following contextual issues.

Defeat and entrapment

Our initial formulation of the SAMS pointed to overlap between concepts, such as defeat, entrapment and hopelessness (Johnson et al., 2008).

Expanding on this, we have argued, on the basis of evidence from a factor analysis of questionnaire measures of defeat and entrapment from samples experiencing psychosis, that these concepts are unitary rather than distinct phenomena (Taylor, Wood, Gooding, Johnson, & Tarrier, 2009). This counters the original position of Gilbert and co-workers who argued that defeat and entrapment had distinct evolutionary functions when examined from a comparative approach that is applicable to humans (Gilbert, 2001, 2006; Gilbert & Gilbert, 2003; Gilbert, Gilbert, & Irons, 2004).

Initially, we assumed prisoners would experience feeling trapped far more intensely that feeling defeated in relation to suicidality. However, a greater appreciation of the personal history of many prisoners enabled us to question this assumption. For example many individuals prior to being imprisoned have been homeless, faced extreme financial hardship, experienced physical, emotional and sexual abuse, and have experienced severe mental health problems (Social Exclusion Unit, 2002). Despite these difficult circumstances, such individuals may have received no help from mental health services or social services. Thus, the prison environment, although harsh, may seem less harsh than the experience of life prior to imprisonment, to someone who has been imprisoned.

With this contextual issue in mind, we examined the extent to which feelings of defeat, entrapment or both predicted the probability of suicide in a sample of 62 current prisoners, who were actively suicidal, using a cross-sectional design. When controlling for depression levels, perceptions of entrapment rather than defeat was a predictor of suicidality (Gooding et al., 2015). The pattern of findings became rather more interesting when we examined ways in which feelings and perceptions of defeat and entrapment interacted with appraisals of coping ability to both exacerbate and ameliorate the probability of suicide in prisoners. As can be seen on the following Figures, low coping ability and high levels of entrapment acted as a risk factor to amplify suicide probability (Figure 3.1). In contrast, low levels of defeat coupled with high levels of coping ability acted to protect prisoners from suicidality (Figure 3.2).

From a clinical perspective, it is important to target perceptions of defeat and entrapment in tandem with perceptions of coping skills but for different reasons. Encouraging low levels of defeat whilst elevating coping skills should protect against suicidality because this combination acts as a resilience factor. Ameliorating high levels of entrapment whilst improving perceived coping skills acts to reduce the high risk of suicide probability that these two factors produce in tandem.

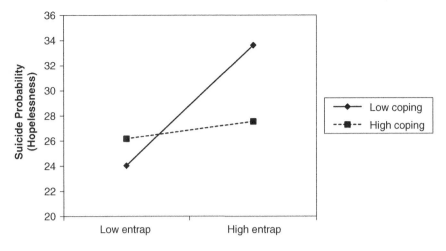

Figure 3.1 Interaction of entrapment and coping skills on the prediction of suicide probability hopelessness

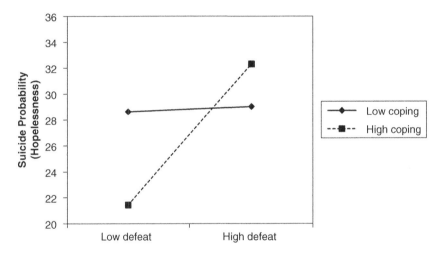

Figure 3.2 Interaction of defeat and coping skills on the prediction of suicide probability hopelessness

Perceptions of social support

There is a wide literature base demonstrating that perceptions of poor social support and social isolation worsen psychological distress and exacerbate mental health problems (Cohen & Wills, 1985; De Silva, McKenzie,

Harpham, & Huttly, 2005; Thoits, 2011). The Interpersonal Theory of Suicide suggests that social reciprocity may play a role in suicidality (Joiner, Van Orden, Witte, & Rudd, 2009). The idea here is that if people feel that they are a burden to friends or family, or a hindrance to society as a whole, then this may worsen feelings of suicidality (Ribeiro & Joiner, 2009). In contrast, if people feel that they can offer social resources of value to others then this may act to give a feeling of self-worth. Indirect evidence for this idea comes from the 'pulling together' effect whereby suicide rates have been found to decrease at the time of positive collective experiences, for example national crises (Joiner, Hollar, & Van Orden, 2007). This idea can be taken further, in that the ability to offer social resources may be seen as a way of legitimising the receipt of reciprocal social support. The improved understanding of the relation between social reciprocity and suicidality warrants further investigation.

In accord with this literature, the SAMS predicts that appraisals of denuded social support and social isolation will amplify suicidality. We conducted an experience sampling study to examine this prediction in 41 prisoners judged to be at risk of suicide. Thus study used a diary method that allowed thoughts and feelings to be examined as they occur "in the moment" (Hektner, Schmidt, & Csikszentmihalyi, 2007). This method is particularly suitable for studying psychopathology because emotions and cognitions are sampled in real time as they occur (Myin-Germeys et al., 2009). In addition to investigating perceptions of social support, we also asked the prisoner participants about social reciprocity. Results were surprising in that *high* levels of social support were associated with *high* levels of suicidal ideation, contrary to what we predicted.

Delineating the mechanisms underlying social support in relation to suicide is complex. This complexity is exacerbated by an environment in which support from other inmates may fluctuate, bullying is rampant, and support from family may serve to remind prisoners of the difficulties that have to be tackled in actually seeing their families in person. Hence, thinking about social support, especially with respect to distant relatives and, at the other end of the scale, bullying inmates, represents numerous complex factors which need to be gauged in future research studies.

One way forward in investigating issues relating to social support and social reciprocity in prisoners is to adopt qualitative methodologies, because this would allow for a richer examination of the subtleties affecting social support for prisoners. However, conducting qualitative interviews within the restrictive and constraining demands of the prison environment and regime also poses its own challenges (see Chapter 8).

References

Bolton, C., Gooding, P., Kapur, N., Barrowclough, C., & Tarrier, N. (2007). Developing psychological perspectives of suicidal behaviour and risk in people with a diagnosis of schizophrenia: We know they kill themselves but do we understand why? *Clinical Psychology Review, 27*(4), 511–536.

Bonta, J., & Gendreau, P. (1990). Reexamining the cruel and unusual punishment of prison life. *Law and Human Behavior, 14*, 347–372.

Brown, G.K., Beck, A.T., Steer, R.A., & Grisham, J.R. (2000). Risk factors for suicide in psychiatric outpatients: A 20-year prospective study. *Journal of Consulting and Clinical Psychology, 68*, 371–377.

Christensen, H., Batterham, P.J., Soubelet, A., & Mackinnon, A.J. (2013). A test of the Interpersonal Theory of Suicide in a large community-based cohort. *Journal of Affective Disorders, 144*(3), 225–234. doi:10.1016/j.jad.2012.07.002

Cohen, S., & Wills, T.A. (1985). Stress, social support, and the buffering hypothesis. *Psychological Bulletin, 98*(2), 310–357.

De Silva, M.J., McKenzie, K., Harpham, T., & Huttly, S.R. (2005). Social capital and mental illness: a systematic review. *Journal of Epidemiology and Community Health, 59*(8), 619–627.

Dhami, M.K., Ayton, P.A., & Loewenstein, G.L. (2007). Adaptation to imprisonment. *Criminal Justice and Behavior, 34*, 1085–1100.

Fawcett, J., Busch, K.A., Jacobs, D., Kravitz, H.M., & Fogg, L. (1997). Suicide: A four-pathway clinical-biochemical model. In D.M. Stoff & J.J. Mann (Eds.), *Neurobiology of suicide – from the bench to the clinic* (pp. 288–301). New York, NY: New York Academy of Sciences.

Gilbert, P. (2001). Evolutionary approaches to psychopathology: The role of natural defences. *Australian and New Zealand Journal of Psychiatry, 35*(1), 17–27.

Gilbert, P. (2006). Evolution and depression: Issues and implications. *Psychological Medicine, 36*(3), 287–297.

Gilbert, P., & Gilbert, J. (2003). Entrapment and arrested fight and flight in depression: An exploration using focus groups. *Psychology and Psychotherapy-Theory Research and Practice, 76*, 173–188.

Gilbert, P., Gilbert, J., & Irons, C. (2004). Life events, entrapments and arrested anger in depression. *Journal of Affective Disorders, 79*(1–3), 149–160.

Gooding, P., Tarrier, N., Dunn, G., Awenat, Y., Shaw, J., Ulph, F., & Pratt, D. (2015). *Psychological characteristics and predictors of suicidal thoughts and behaviours in high risk prisoners.* Manuscript submitted for publication.

Granello, D.H. (2010). The process of suicide risk assessment: Twelve core principles. *Journal of Counseling & Development, 88*(3), 363–370.

Gunnel, D., Harbord, R., Singleton, N., Jenkins, R., & Lewis, G. (2004). Factors influencing the development and amelioration of suicidal thoughts in the general population. *British Journal of Psychiatry, 185*, 385–393.

Gunnel, D., Saperia, J., & Ashby, D. (2005). Selective serotonin reuptake inhibitors (SSRIs) and suicide in adults: Meta-analysis of drug company data from placebo controlled, randomised controlled trials submitted to the MHRA's safety review. *British Medical Journal, 330*(7488), 385–390.

Haney, C. (2003). The psychological impact of incarceration: implications for post-prison adjustment. In J. Travis & M. Waul (Eds.), *Prisoners once removed: The impact of incarceration and re-entry on children, families, and communities.* (pp. 33–66). Washington, DC: Urban Institute.

Harvey, J. (2007). *Young men in prison: Surviving and adapting to life inside.* Cullompton, Devon: Willan.

Hawton, K., Casañas i Comabella, C., Haw, C., & Saunders, K. (2013). Risk factors for suicide in individuals with depression: A systematic review. *Journal of Affective Disorders, 147*(1–3), 17–28. doi:10.1016/j.jad.2013.01.004

Hawton, K., & van Heeringen, K. (2009). Suicide. *Lancet, 373*(9672), 1372–1381.

Hektner, J.M., Schmidt, J.A. and Csikszentmihalyi, M. (Eds.). (2007). *Experience sampling method: Measuring the quality of everyday life.* London, UK: Sage.

Johnson, J., Gooding, P., & Tarrier, N. (2008). Suicide risk in schizophrenia: Explanatory models and clinical implications, the schematic appraisal model of suicide (SAMS). *Psychology and Psychotherapy-Theory Research and Practice, 81,* 55–77.

Johnson, M.M., & Rhodes, R. (2008). Institutionalization: A theory of human behavior and the social environment. *Advances in Social Work, 8,* 219–236.

Joiner, T.E., Hollar, D., & Van Orden, K.A. (2007). On Buckeyes, Gators, Super Bowl Sunday, and the Miracle on Ice: "Pulling together" is associated with lower suicide rates. *Journal of Social and Clinical Psychology, 25,* 180–196.

Joiner, T.E., Van Orden, K.A., Witte, T.K., & Rudd, M.D. (2009). *The interpersonal theory of suicide: Guidance for working with suicidal clients.* Washington, DC: American Psychological Association.

Joiner, T.E., Van Orden, K.A., Witte, T.K., Selby, E.A., Ribeiro, J.D., Lewis, R., & Rudd, M.D. (2009). Main predictions of the interpersonal-psychological theory of suicidal behavior: Empirical tests in two samples of young adults. *Journal of Abnormal Psychology, 118*(3), 634–646.

Joormann, J., & D'Avanzato, C. (2010). Emotion regulation in depression: Examining the role of cognitive processes. *Cognition & Emotion, 24*(6), 913–939. doi:10.1080/02699931003784939

Kessler, R.C., Chiu W.T., Demler, O., Merikangas, K.R., & Walters, E.E. (2005). Prevalence, severity, and comorbidity of 12-month *DSM-IV* disorders in the National Comorbidity Survey Replication. *Archives of General Psychiatry, 62*(6), 617–627. doi:10.1001/archpsyc.62.6.617

Kessler, R.C., Ormel, J., Petukhova, M., McLaughlin, K.A., Grief Green, J., Russo, L.J., . . . Ustün, T.B. (2011). Development of lifetime comorbidity in the World Health Organization world mental health surveys. *Archives of General Psychiatry, 68*(1), 90–100. doi:10.1001/archgenpsychiatry.2010.180

Klewchuk, E.M., McCusker, C.G., Mulholland, C., & Shannon, C. (2007). Cognitive biases for trauma stimuli in people with schizophrenia. *British Journal of Clinical Psychology, 46,* 333–345. doi:10.1348/014466507x173385

MacLeod, A.K., Rose, G.S., & Williams, J.M.G. (1993). Components of hopelessness about the future in parasuicide. *Cognitive Therapy and Research, 17*(5), 441–455.

Morrison, R., & O'Connor, R.C. (2008). The role of rumination, attentional biases and stress in psychological distress. *British Journal of Psychology, 99,* 191–209.

Myin-Germeys, I., Oorschot, M., Collip, D., Lataster, J., Delespaul, P., & van Os, J. (2009). Experience sampling research in psychopathology: Opening the black box of daily life. *Psychological Medicine, 39*(09), 1533–1547.

National Institute for Health and Care Excellence. (2011). *Self-harm: Longer-term management* (Clinical guideline CG133). Available from http://guidance.nice.org. uk/CG133

O'Connor, R. C., & Cassidy, C. (2007). Predicting hopelessness: The interaction between optimism/pessimism and specific future expectancies. *Cognition and Emotion, 21*(3), 596–613.

O'Connor, R. C., & Nock, M. K. (2014). The psychology of suicidal behaviour. *Lancet Psychiatry, 1*(1), 73–85. doi:10.1016/S2215-0366(14)70222-6

Panagioti, M., Gooding, P., Dunn, G., & Tarrier, N. (2011). Pathways to suicidal behavior in posttraumatic stress disorder. *Journal of Traumatic Stress, 24*(2), 137–145. doi:10.1002/jts.20627

Panagioti, M., Gooding, P. A., & Tarrier, N. (2012). Hopelessness, defeat, and entrapment in posttraumatic stress disorder their association with suicidal behavior and severity of depression. *Journal of Nervous and Mental Disease, 200*(8), 676–683. doi:10.1097/NMD.0b013e3182613f91

Panagioti, M., Gooding, P., & Tarrier, N. (2015). A prospective study of suicidal ideation in posttraumatic stress disorder: The role of perceptions of defeat and entrapment. *Journal of Clinical Psychology, 71*(1), 50–61.

Panagioti, M., Gooding, P., Taylor, P. J., & Tarrier, N. (2014). Perceived social support buffers the impact of PTSD symptoms on suicidal behavior: implications into suicide resilience research. *Comprehensive Psychiatry, 55*(1), 104–112. doi:10.1016/j. comppsych.2013.06.004

Ribeiro, J. D., & Joiner, T. E. (2009). The interpersonal-psychological theory of suicidal behavior: Current status and future directions. *Journal of Clinical Psychology, 65*(12), 1291–1299.

Sachs-Ericsson, N., Hames, J. L., Joiner, T. E., Corsentino, E., Rushing, N. C., Palmer, E., & Steffens, D. C. (2014). Differences between suicide attempters and nonattempters in depressed older patients: Depression severity, white-matter lesions, and cognitive functioning. *American Journal of Geriatric Psychiatry, 22*(1), 75–85. doi:10.1016/j.jagp.2013.01.063

Selby, E. A., & Joiner, T. E., Jr. (2013). Emotional cascades as prospective predictors of dysregulated behaviors in borderline personality disorder. *Personality Disorders-Theory Research and Treatment, 4*(2), 168–174. doi:10.1037/a0029933

Shneidman, E. S. (1993). Commentary: Suicide as psychache. *The Journal of Nervous and Mental Disease, 181*(3), 145–147.

Social Exclusion Unit. (2002). *Reducing re-offending by ex-prisoners.* London, UK: Author.

Tarrier, N., Gooding, P., Pratt, D., Kelly, J., Awenat, Y., & Maxwell, J. (2013). *Cognitive behavioural prevention of suicide in psychosis: A treatment manual.* London, UK: Routledge.

Tarrier, N., Kelly, J., Maqsood, S., Snelson, N., Maxwell, J., Law, H., Gooding, P. (2014). The cognitive behavioural prevention of suicide in psychosis: A clinical trial. *Schizophrenia Research, 156*(2–3), 204–210. doi:10.1016/j.schres.2014.04.029

Taylor, J. L., & John, C. H. (2004). Attentional and memory bias in persecutory delusions and depression. *Psychopathology, 37*(5), 233–241. doi:10.1159/000080719

Taylor, P. J., Gooding, P. A., Wood, A. M., & Tarrier, N. (2010). Memory specificity as a risk factor for suicidality in non-affective psychosis: The ability to recall specific autobiographical memories is related to greater suicidality. *Behaviour Research and Therapy, 48*(10), 1047–1052. doi:10.1016/j.brat.2010.06.001

Taylor, P. J., Gooding, P., Wood, A. M., & Tarrier, N. (2011). The role of defeat and entrapment in depression, anxiety, and suicide. *Psychological Bulletin, 137*(3), 391–420. doi:10.1037/a0022935

Taylor, P. J., Wood, A. M., Gooding, P., Johnson, J., & Tarrier, N. (2009). Are defeat and entrapment best defined as a single construct? *Personality and Individual Differences, 47*(7), 795–797.

Thoits, P. A. (2011). Mechanisms linking social ties and support to physical and mental health. *Journal of Health and Social Behavior, 52*(2), 145–161.

Van Orden, K. A., Witte, T. K., Cukrowicz, K. C., Braithwaite, S. R., Selby, E. A., & Joiner, T. E. (2010). The interpersonal theory of suicide. *Psychological Review, 117*(2), 575–600.

Whittington, C. J., Kendall, T., Fonagy, P., Cottrell, D., Cotgrove, A., & Boddington, E. (2004). Selective serotonin reuptake inhibitors in childhood depression: Systematic review of published versus unpublished data. *Lancet, 363*(9418), 1341–1345.

Williams, M. (1997). *Cry of pain: Understanding suicide and self-harm.* London, UK: Harmondsworth Penguin.

Young, M. A., Fogg, L. F., Scheftner, W., Fawcett, J., Akiskal, H., & Maser, J. (1996). Stable trait components of hopelessness: baseline and sensitivity to depression. *Journal of Abnormal Psychology, 105*(2), 155–165.

4   Cognitive behaviour therapy for suicidal prisoners

Daniel Pratt

Psychological interventions for prisoners

There exists a wide gap between the large demand for but limited supply of psychological interventions for prisoners (Brooker & Gojkovic, 2009). Adjusting to prison life tends to be a difficult and demanding process. For many prisoners, imprisonment presents practical, social, and psychological challenges and can be destabilising with "fear, anxiety, loneliness, trauma, depression, injustice, powerlessness, violence and uncertainty all part of the experience of prison life" (Liebling & Maruna, 2005, p. 3).

Although prisoners are identified as a high-risk group for suicide, there are no evidence-based psychological interventions to prevent suicidality for this group. Prisoners and their families are a significant part of the socially excluded population (Murray, 2007; Social Exclusion Unit, 2002). As emphasised in international and national policies, imprisonment, therefore, offers an opportunity to address the pre-existing unmet health needs of this 'hard to reach' sector of society (Department of Health and HM Prison Service, 2002; US Department of Health and Human Sciences, 2001; World Health Organization, 2008). Pompili et al (2009) highlighted prison and jail settings should provide staff training, reception screening protocols, improved staff communication, documentations and internal resources, in addition to improving access to mental health treatments for offenders identified as at risk of suicidal behaviour. Each of these practices is unlikely to achieve much success if implemented in isolation; rather, an integrated programme exerting influence over prisoners' entire pathway through the prison system is more likely to be effective.

A general consensus has developed that suicidal behaviour in prisons is caused by an interaction of vulnerabilities that prisoners bring with them ('import') from society into the establishments (e.g. previous psychological problems, history of self-harm, substance misuse issues), and the deprivation endured by the prisoner whilst in custody (Harvey, 2007; Liebling, Durie, Stiles, & Tait, 2005). Prisoner distress develops as a result of the interaction between levels of pre-existing 'imported vulnerability' with 'relational dimensions' such as prisoner-staff relationships, respect, perceived fairness and dignity (Liebling et al., 2005). Such an interaction highlights the importance of the prison environment in the well-being of prisoners. For example, 'vulnerable' prisoners are more easily distressed by the negative effects of imprisonment, but may also be open to the rehabilitative effects of the positive aspects of prison life, such as time out of cell, employment, association time with peers and contact with family members. The ongoing and relentless impact of the prison environment on the vulnerable prisoner at risk of suicide must always come into consideration when attempting to offer psychological interventions to such individuals (Harvey, 2011).

A growing number of jails and prisons have developed comprehensive suicide prevention programs alongside national standards and guidelines for prison suicide prevention (Konrad et al., 2007). Approaches to the prevention of suicide can be categorised into primary prevention and secondary prevention strategies (Hanson, 2010). Primary strategies target environmental factors that could have an effect on the overall incidence of suicide in prisons, for example policies and procedures, staffing practices and the physical design of the establishment. Secondary strategies focus on ways to intervene with offenders considered to be at high risk of suicide, for example counselling, peer support and prisoner observation aides.

The central component of most prison suicide prevention programs is a care-planning system operated by multi-disciplinary staff teams providing individualised care for prisoners at risk of suicidal behaviour (Daigle et al, 2007; HM Prison Service, 2005; International Association for Correctional and Forensic Psychology Practice Standards Committee, 2010). Protocols tend to specify provision of staff training, prisoner screening at reception, assessment, ongoing monitoring and management, treatment and follow-up. Such systems are used both for crisis intervention and to help prisoners cope with longer term problems. In the UK, over 1,500 prisoners (approximately 2% of prison population) are identified under the suicide risk management system on any one day (Ministry of Justice, 2011), with each at-risk prisoner offered an assessment, ongoing monitoring and generic counselling.

Coping with a prison environment that embodies fear, distrust and a lack of control can leave prisoners feeling overwhelmed and hopeless, leading some of them to choose suicide as a way to escape. Currently, intervention efforts target environmental factors by introducing changes to the prison environment and regime, or by increasing assessment and monitoring practices. Such efforts continue to be made within prison systems although the effectiveness of these interventions remains unclear (Hayes, 2010). Insufficient access is provided to evidence-based psychological interventions to support prisoners in the development of coping strategies when experiencing such distress associated with future suicidality.

Psychological interventions for suicidality

Systematic reviews of psychological interventions have reported efficacy in the reduction of repetition of suicidal behaviour and self-harm (Crawford, Thomas, Khan, & Kulinskaya, 2007; Mann et al, 2005). Cognitive behavior therapy (CBT), problem-solving therapy and interpersonal therapy were highlighted to be the most promising interventions (Gaynes et al., 2004; Mann et al., 2005) with CBT shown to halve the reattempt rate, compared with usual treatment alone (Brown et al., 2005).

In a review and meta-analysis of 25 studies of cognitive behavioural interventions for suicide behaviour, a highly significant overall effect was reported (Tarrier, Taylor, and Gooding, 2008). The review highlighted group CBT interventions were ineffective, whereas individual sessions alone or when coupled with group sessions were highly effective. Importantly, CBT was found to be effective only when the therapy was directly focused upon the prevention of suicidal behaviour, whereas suicide prevention viewed as a secondary gain within the treatment of another mental health problem, for example CBT for depression or psychosis, was ineffective.

Since the Tarrier et al. (2008) review, this evidence base has continued to become more established. In a trial of 10 sessions of cognitive therapy following a recent suicide attempt, relative to participants receiving usual care, CBT recipients were 50% less likely to re-engage in suicide behaviour in the subsequent 18 months and achieved significant improvements on measures of depression and hopelessness and the rate of recovery for problem-solving skills (Brown et al., 2005; Ghahramanlou-Holloway, Bhar, Brown, Olson, & Beck, 2012). Similarly, in a sample of 90 patients presenting to a local medical centre following suicidal behaviour, those randomised to receiving 12 sessions of CBT reported significantly reduced levels of suicidal ideation, improved problem-solving ability and improved self-esteem, compared with the standard care group (Slee, Garnefski, van der Leeden, Arensman, & Spinhoven, 2008).

CBT for suicidal prisoners

To date, the development of CBT approaches for the prevention of suicide has not been extended into working with vulnerable prisoners, despite the exaggerated rates of suicide in this high-risk group. Indeed, prisoners' access to psychological interventions for mental health problems has generally been found to be largely absent (Department of Health, 2009). This may seem surprising considering the prevalent use of cognitive behavioural programmes for the reduction of re-conviction and recidivism of offending behaviours.

Previous reviews and meta-analyses of offender behaviour programmes, focused on reducing criminal recidivism, have shown prisoner interventions to be most effective when they have been well-designed, targeted and systematically delivered with cognitive-behavioural approaches a particularly successful type of intervention for offenders (Gendreau, 1996; Lipsey, Landenberger, & Wilson, 2007; McDougall, Perry, Calrbour, Bowles, & Worthy, 2009; McGuire, 2002). Drawing upon this supportive evidence of the feasibility and acceptability of CBT for the prevention of criminal behaviour to prisoners, and also the preliminary support for CBT for suicidal behaviour (albeit outside of offender groups), there is reason to be optimistic that a CBT for the prevention of suicide could be feasibly delivered within the context of a prison setting and offer considerable clinical benefit to the most vulnerable prisoner patients.

Cognitive Behavioural Suicide Prevention therapy

Overview of CBSP

During the last seven or so years, our Understanding the Psychology of Suicide (UPSide) research group at the University of Manchester has developed the Cognitive Behavioral Suicide Prevention (CBSP) therapy that offers a structured, theoretically based intervention designed to address and amend the specific psychological architecture responsible for suicidal behaviour, using established cognitive-behavioural techniques (see Tarrier et al., 2013 for treatment manual). In brief, the CBSP therapy aims to have an impact upon the processes proposed to be involved in suicidal behaviour, according to the Schematic Appraisal Model of Suicide (SAMS; Johnson, Gooding, & Tarrier, 2008). This model has been empirically validated in suicidal persons experiencing psychosis (Taylor et al., 2010) and post-traumatic stress disorder (Panagioti, Gooding, Taylor, & Tarrier, 2012).

The CBSP treatment protocol systematically addresses pertinent cognitive mechanisms in a tiered approach, moving from attentional processes to appraisals and then onto schematic processes (Tarrier et al., 2013). This is done in tandem with strategies derived from Broaden & Build principles (Fredrickson & Branigan, 2005). These strategies aim to disrupt the stronghold of threat activation on attention, appraisals and the suicide schema, assisted by the stimulation of positive affect, in order to increase psychological resilience. It is also intended to increase positive goal-seeking motivations; the development of which are thought to reduce the scope and influence of the suicide schema on a person's functioning.

CBSP draws on traditional CBT (Beck, 1976; Wenzel, Brown, & Beck, 2009) but is distinctive in that is also aims to identify and amplify the processes that allow a person to deactivate the suicide schema and activate alternative and more functional thoughts, behaviours and feelings. Also, CBSP stimulates positive emotion with the purpose of the inhibition of threat-related processes. Tarrier (2010) developed the Broad Minded Affective Coping (BMAC) technique to enable clients to gain easier access to positive experiences of coping and problem solving, which may result in a greater sense of personal achievement and self-efficacy, improved control over positive and negative emotions and an awareness of the relationship between cognitions and emotions.

Delivery of CBSP

The CBSP intervention is typically delivered over a four- to six-month period, with clients offered up to 20 individual sessions lasting 30 to 60 minutes, on a once- or twice-weekly basis. Initial sessions focus on engagement and assessment of the participants' presenting problems, previous experiences of suicidal ideation and behaviour and formulation of key areas for intervention. During intermediate sessions, the participant is supported in developing a set of helpful skills and strategies to improve coping and enhance resilience towards suicide behaviour. The final phase of the treatment is the development of a 'maintaining well-being' plan or therapy blueprint that serves as a summary of work completed. Each of these phases will now be described in more detail.

Engagement and assessment

A comprehensive assessment is undertaken which aims to identify the participant's current level of risk in order to inform risk management, to gather information about factors which may contribute to the participant's vulnerability to suicide and to identify factors that may be harnessed to reduce vulnerability and improve resilience. In addition to the participant's self-report, and with his or her informed consent, the therapist gathers information from those significant others who are also involved in the participant's ongoing care and support, which tends to comprise prison and probation staff, healthcare professionals, and family members where contact has been maintained.

Drawing together the information gathered during the assessment phase, a personalised case formulation is then collaboratively developed. The formulation seeks to incorporate relevant material from the participant's previous life experiences, core beliefs about suicide and what suicide means to him or her, key appraisals of the individual's situation, self-perceptions, and the subsequent emotional, behavioural and cognitive responses to suicidal behaviour.

Once the client and therapist have discussed the formulation and made refinements where necessary, the goals for therapy can then be discussed. Identifying goals for change can be a difficult challenge for those clients who are particularly pessimistic about their future and the likelihood of anything worthwhile coming from their involvement in the treatment (Britton, Williams, & Conner, 2008). In such circumstances, the therapist can present the treatment as a 'no-lose' situation, in which the client simply has to be willing to try the therapy for a few weeks before making any firmer commitment to continue. Collaboratively agreed goals then inform the development of the treatment plan and the prioritising of the subsequent intervention modules.

Treatment

Following the assessment and conceptualisation of the client's suicidal experiences, a treatment plan is developed that targets up to five key suicidal processes. Throughout treatment, a range of cognitive and behavioural techniques are introduced in accord with the target processes. The therapist may find it helpful to initially model the use of each technique to ensure the client has a sufficient understanding to allow them to practice the technique as a homework task.

The five modules within the CBSP treatment programme are as follows:

- Attentional control training
- Appraisal restructuring
- Problem-solving skills training
- Behavioural activation
- Schema-focused techniques

Attentional control training ('getting control of my thinking')

According to the SAMS (Johnson et al., 2008), in times of a suicidal crisis, individuals tend to become 'locked in' to a pattern of suicide ideation that they believe to be difficult to control. With the suicide schema activated, the individual's attention becomes overly focused upon identifying potential threats in his or her environment, and even non-threatening stimuli becomes interpreted as dangerous. Hence, the first stage of CBSP is to reduce the valence of threat-focused attention and other information-processing biases that maintain the activation of the suicide schema. CBSP uses an attention-training technique (Wells, 2009) to help reduce the participant's excessive tendency to focus upon threat- and suicide-related stimuli (both internal and external).

Through the use of the attention training technique, clients learn how to overcome 'attentional fixation' by switching their attention onto non-self-relevant aspects of their environment, with the initial focus of the technique on sounds from various spatial locations. The technique is then extended to include attention to imagery, with initial practice focused on visual objects within the client's immediate environment, such as a mug on a shelf, before practising focusing attention upon neutrally valenced internal images, such as waiting in the dinner queue. Through continued practice, clients develop a broader sense of their experiences and the world around them, despite the presence of distressing thoughts, and gain a greater sense of control over whether to engage with the interfering cognitions.

Attentional control can then be further strengthened using the BMAC technique (Tarrier, 2010). In the BMAC technique, the client is initially asked to think about a memory related to a positive event from his or her past, typically a family event, birthday party, wedding day. To begin the technique, the client is asked to relax through a brief breathing exercise, and then to bring to mind an image of his or her preferred positive memory. Whilst maintaining the image in his or her attention, the client is invited to fully engage with the memory across all senses. So the client is prompted to move around the image and focus in on the visual details (e.g. objects, people, background) and then observe any sounds from various locations within the scene. The client is then prompted to bring to life the recalled memory through any related sensations of touch, smell or taste. Through recalling sensory details and sustaining the memory in his or her attention, the client is then instructed to recall positive feelings he or she experiences at the time of the memory and then to bring these emotions back to life in the present moment – to re-experience the positive affect in the here and now. Subsequent questioning by the therapist helps the client to identify any positive meaning attached to this emotion and the implications for the client's sense of control over his or her attention and associated feelings.

Appraisal restructuring ('challenging unhelpful thinking')

According to the SAMS, a number of key appraisals are maintained by the suicidal individual that need to be identified and challenged through traditional cognitive methods. Specific appraisals often concern the client's current situation in prison, past events often related to offending or drug-related behaviours and negative predictions for the future. Furthermore, client distress can also stem from a fragmented sense of self, low perceived personal agency and little confidence in his or her ability to effect positive changes in the future. Initially, psychoeducation work focuses on improving the client's awareness of common thinking biases, for example selective abstraction/negative mental filter, magnification/catastrophising and arbitrary inference/jumping to conclusions (Williams & Garland, 2002). When sufficiently familiar with such biases, the client begins to monitor occurrences of any such unhelpful thinking styles within his or her daily experiences. The accuracy and likelihood of the client's appraisals is then considered by encouraging him or her to evaluate the evidence for and against the thought. Where possible, behavioural experiments are used to encourage the client to seek out and identify disconfirmatory evidence directly. Any new evidence can then be considered to challenge the accuracy and usefulness of any unhelpful beliefs.

Problem-solving skills training ('solving problems')

Because deficits in interpersonal problem-solving are associated with suicidality (Pollock & Williams, 1998), a structured technique to developing skills in improving solving such problems is included within the therapy. The CBSP intervention proposes the following approach to problem-solving training:

1   List clearly the problem(s) to be resolved
2   Select a problem and clearly and simply define it
3   Brainstorm as many solutions as possible
4   List the advantages and disadvantages of each possible solution
5   Select and implement a solution
6   Evaluate the effectiveness of the selected solution. If ineffective, select and implement an alternative solution, and repeat.

It can be helpful for clients to learn the steps of this technique on a hypothetical, everyday problem, for example "You have a headache and would like paracetamol". In this example, the therapist would use a Socratic questioning style to support the client to arrange hypothetical access to non-prescription medication through the usual prison application procedure.

When confidence in the use of the technique is developed, the client is then encouraged to apply the technique to his or her own previous problems related to suicidal distress. This approach thus helps clients to learn how the technique may have helped them to consider alternative responses to suicide behaviours. To extend the use of this technique further, the client can consider potential problems likely to affect him or her in the future and then work through the aforementioned steps again to develop plans of how to resolve the problem should it actually occur. Self-reflections on the client's use of the problem-solving techniques are then used to inform the development of more positive appraisals of coping in future situations, such as "When I think problems through, I am able to find solutions," and "I am learning how to cope better when I'm facing a problem."

Behavioural activation ('living a life worth living')

An effective behavioural technique when working with a depressed or suicidal participant is behavioural activation (Dimidjian, et al., 2006; Jacobson, Martell, & Dimidjian, 2001). The sense of inertia that a state of hopelessness, defeat or entrapment often leaves an individual with can be challenged using regular self-monitoring of the client's activities of daily living (Beck & Greenberg, 1974). Activities found to be associated with an increased sense of pleasure, achievement or both are timetabled into the client's daily or weekly schedule. The resulting increase in time spent accessing pleasurable or achievement activities can elevate the client's engagement with their external environment, such as time spent with peers, family and friends, and ensure routine access to positive, alternative schema that would strengthen the client's resilience, sense of personal agency and control over his or her life (Tarrier et al., 2013; Wenzel et al., 2009). This improved sense of meaning in the client's life and increased connection with his or her social network serves to undermine the potential 'no rescue' appraisals, such as "I'm alone, and no one will help me" (Johnson et al., 2008; Williams & Pollock, 2000). In prison, the client's access to pleasurable activities is often considerably compromised, which requires the therapist to support the client to focus on realistically achievable activities, for example watching TV, listening to music, reading a book, visiting the gym, talking to a friend and walking with peers in the exercise yard. Despite such limitations, the basic premise of the technique – engaging more in pleasurable or achievement activities serves to improve mood – remains a realistic goal for this phase of therapy.

Schema-focused techniques ('improving my self-esteem')

The final component of a client's treatment plan focuses upon the suicide schema. The aim for this phase is to deactivate, inhibit or change the suicide-related schema through the adoption of new and appropriate schematic beliefs about the client's circumstances, self and future. Reduced activation of the suicide schema can be achieved through the enhancement of more positive schemas with associated links with more adaptive problem-solving responses. Methods are used that help to promote positive self-worth, for example the client is supported to draw up a list of 10 positive qualities about himself or herself, each of these qualities are then rated as to how much the client believes they are actually true. The client is then invited to recollect specific examples of when he or she demonstrated each quality, with detailed memories then used as examples for BMAC practices between sessions. This practice is intended to emphasise and bolster the client's memories of positive experiences. Re-ratings of the client's belief in each of the positive qualities are then used to develop the client's awareness of his or her beliefs changing according to what evidence he or she focuses attention upon. The client can then be supported to develop an implementable plan of preferred goals and ambitions for the future, especially for when released from prison and back with his or her family. This serves to build hope for the future and is intended to provoke a reason for living despite current distress and hardship.

Maintaining well-being plans

Typically in the final two or three sessions, the client develops a plan for how he or she intends to maintain any gains in his or her sense of well-being achieved during the course of therapy. The focus of the plan is to summarise key lessons learnt from the treatment and to identify both new coping techniques and strategies now available to the client and additional sources of support within the community (peers, staff, family). Key high-risk situations of potential future suicidal crises are identified, and the client is encouraged to imagine how he or she would use any new skills learnt during therapy or external resources to overcome, or at least manage, the distress associated with the crisis.

Preliminary results for CBSP

CBSP therapy for participants living in the community has previously been evaluated in a randomised controlled trial of 50 suicidal patients experiencing psychosis, relative to a control group receiving treatment as usual (Tarrier et al., 2014). Those allocated to the treatment group received up to 24 sessions of CBSP and were found to be significantly superior on measures of suicide probability, suicidal ideation and hopelessness compared with the treatment as usual group. This study makes an encouraging contribution to the evidence base for CBSP, but how does this intervention translate into the prison environment? Is it possible to deliver similar therapeutic benefit to suicidal prisoners?

These questions have recently been answered in a new randomised controlled trial of CBSP therapy for suicidal prisoners (Pratt et al., in press). The primary aim of the Prevention of Suicide in Prisons (PROSPeR) study was to examine the feasibility and acceptability of delivering and evaluating CBSP therapy to prisoners identified under the Asessment, Care in Custody and Teamwork (ACCT) system as presenting a risk to themselves. A secondary aim was to develop preliminary estimates of the impact of this therapy on suicidality and related psychological variables within a male prisoner sample in England.

Sixty-two prisoner participants took part in the trial, with half allocated to receiving the usual support under the ACCT system and half receiving the CBSP therapy in addition to usual support. Participants were typical of the male prisoner population, with a mean age of 35 years ($SD = 11.1$), 86% were white British, and 57% were single. To meet eligibility criteria for the trial, all prisoners had been identified under the ACCT system during the month prior to entry to the study. There was substantial experience of suicidal behaviour amongst the 62 participants, with only 9 (15%) prisoners having not previously attempted suicide compared with 35 (56%) participants who had made multiple previous attempts.

The feasibility of delivering CBSP therapy to prisoners was examined in terms of engagement and retention in the intervention. Overall, engagement was found to be good with an average of 9 therapy sessions attended per participant in the treatment arm of the trial. Only 16 of 276 (6%) of sessions were refused, suggesting the participants benefitted from the sessions and attached value to their continued attendance. Therapist ratings were collected to provide a further indication of engagement and participation with the CBSP therapy programme. Ratings for promptness, attendance and level of client participation were above the mid-point of the scale, and ratings for disruptive behaviour were very low, all of which indicates the therapy was generally acceptable to prisoners.

In terms of outcomes, CBSP therapy was found to have a beneficial impact upon the incidence of suicidal behaviour. Compared with the control group of prisoners receiving routine support alone, prisoners who also received the CBSP therapy were less than half as likely to engage in self-injurious behaviour. Furthermore, there was a consistent pattern that recipients of CBSP therapy made greater levels of improvement on self-report questionnaire measures of suicidal ideation, depression, hopelessness and self-esteem. Significant improvements were also found on measures of psychiatric symptomatology and personality dysfunction. Importantly, the CBSP therapy was found to be associated with a significant increase in the number of participants achieving a clinically significant recovery in terms of returning to the non-clinical range on a measure of suicidal probability by the end of therapy.

Although this study was exploratory in nature, in order to assess the potential of CBSP therapy for prisoners, these results provide a firm indication that the therapy can be feasibly delivered to vulnerable prisoners. Recipients successfully engage in the therapy programme, which offers substantial promise as an effective intervention that provides clinical benefit to prisoners in terms of reduced suicidal behaviour and improved psychological well-being. This small-scale pilot justifies the need for further investigation of the effectiveness of CBSP for prisoners, in the form of a larger scale, multi-site randomised controlled trial.

Case example of CBSP therapy for a suicidal prisoner

With CBSP holding the potential to be an effective treatment for the prevention of suicide behaviour, we now provide an example of how CBSP therapy was delivered with a young male prisoner who staff considered to be at high risk of suicide. This case example was a participant in the therapy arm of the randomised controlled trial described earlier, and is presented here to highlight our experiences of working with this clinical group. Of specific interest in this case example is an examination of the pattern of changes in relation to suicidal thoughts and ideation, risk of future suicide behaviour and related psychological distress, such as hopelessness, associated with this intervention. This case example demonstrates the experiences, benefits and challenges faced by the vulnerable prisoner, and hopefully provokes reflection by the reader on the obstacles that have to be overcome by the client and therapist when undertaking this work. Some identifying details of the case have been altered to preserve confidentiality.

Introducing Mark

Mark was a 22-year-old white British male with a history of depression and anxiety problems and was currently prescribed anti-depressant medication from the prison GP and was receiving regular contact with the Mental Health In-Reach Team in the prison. Mark described his childhood as chaotic and unpredictable. He had a younger brother but no recollection of his father who had left the family home when Mark was 2 years old and his mother was pregnant with his younger brother. Mark's mother was a long-term user of illicit drugs for most of his upbringing. Mark reported frequent episodes of his mother being 'out of it', leaving him to cook, clean and care for his brother. At the age of 14 years, Mark's mother left the family home and Mark assumed the role of carer for his younger brother. Mark recalled feeling 'abandoned' by his mother and then responsible for his brother's well-being, which led him to develop a core belief of 'I am unlovable' and a conditional assumption of 'To be happy, I have to be with someone I love'. Following his mother's departure, Mark began to engage in gang-related criminal behaviour to earn a living. Mark received several Anti-Social Behaviour Orders (ASBOs) before his first prison sentence at the age of 18 years for a robbery offence, serving two years in prison. Within four months of his release, Mark was remanded back into custody for a new offence of aggravated robbery. Mark had been imprisoned for seven months at the time of his referral to the study and was fearful of a potential seven-year sentence in connection with the violent nature of the robbery. Mark's court case was expected to be heard in nine months' time. Mark attended therapy over a period of four months, during which time he attended 19 sessions, was unable to attend a further 5 sessions because of legal visits and chose not to attend 1 session.

At the time of referral into the study, Mark had been in a relationship with his girlfriend for approximately one year, and she had recently had their first child. Mark received regular visits from his girlfriend but was becoming increasingly worried that she would leave him if he continued to spend time in prison and away from their home. Previously, when Mark had been in prison, an ex-girlfriend had ended her relationship with Mark, stating she wanted to be with someone else (outside of prison).

During the current prison term, Mark reported he had harmed himself on five previous occasions, each time by cutting his upper arms or chest. Initial sessions focused on the collaborative development of

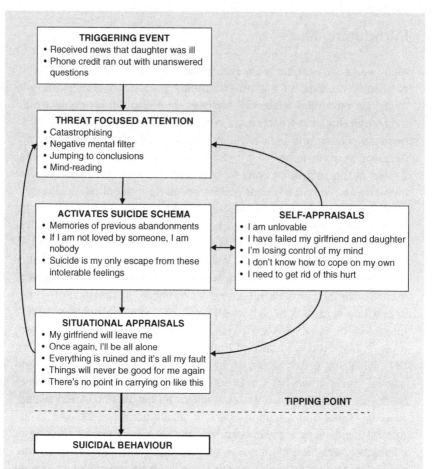

Figure 4.1 Formulation for Mark

a formulation of Mark's most recent suicide behavior, which occurred three weeks prior to the start of therapy (see Figure 4.1). Mark reported he had received news from his girlfriend that his daughter was ill and had needed to be admitted to hospital. Mark had received this news in a brief phone call with his girlfriend that was ended abruptly as Mark had run out of credit on the prison telephone. Mark was left with a number of questions and worries about his daughter's ill-health but with no access to any immediate answers because his phone account could not be credited again until the following week. Upon returning to his cell after the phone call, Mark described how he began to 'lose control of my mind', with his anxious thoughts spiralling into greater catastrophes linked to the belief of 'I am unlovable'. Within a couple of days, Mark had become convinced that his girlfriend would leave him for someone who could provide care and support to her and their daughter. With such an imagined future considered indubitable, Mark predicted he would be abandoned again, which would lead to terrible feelings of loneliness. Becoming increasingly hopeless activated beliefs that 'there's no point in doing anything to stop this' and 'everything is ruined, and it's all my fault'. At this time, Mark withdrew from his daily activities and chose to spend more of his time in his cell away from others. Mark's feelings of despair and defeat grew into a realisation that ending his life was the only solution to his situation. Mark secured a blade from another prisoner on the wing and cut himself on the upper chest during the night time. The next morning, Mark was assessed by the healthcare staff and considered to be not requiring further medical assistance because the injury was reported as 'superficial'. Hearing this description, Mark appraised his suicide attempt as yet another example of his continuing failures ("I can't even kill myself properly!").

Mark considered his use of self-harm to be unhelpful in the long-term and served to maintain his self-critical beliefs and underlying low self-esteem. The goals for therapy were to improve Mark's response to problematic social/interpersonal situations and to enhance Mark's ability to manage intense emotions and stress.

Mark expressed a willingness to engage in practically focused techniques, and so a series of problem-solving training sessions began the intervention phase of the therapy. Mark was instructed in how to use a systematic approach to problem solving. Initial examples of everyday problems were used to enable Mark to familiarise himself and rehearse the new skills (e.g. wanting to read the newspaper but out of credit). Later sessions drew upon more recent scenarios that had caused Mark to become distressed, such as being refused access to the gym. Through the completion of structured worksheets between sessions, Mark internalised the steps of the process. The application of this technique was then extended to hypothetical scenarios that were similar to Mark's previous suicidal crises (e.g. girlfriend 'dumps' me over the phone). Future or potential high-risk situations were also worked through to support the integration of the new skills into Mark's repertoire of coping strategies.

The next phase of therapy enabled Mark to challenge some of the catastrophic predictions and worries he often experienced when in a highly distressed state. Through the completion of thought diary records, both in session and as homework tasks, Mark developed a systematic approach to 'thinking about my thinking', which encouraged him to access more rational alternatives to the worst case scenario often predicted.

The final phase of the therapy work was focused on improving Mark's self-esteem. Enhanced access to more positive schema was achieved through supporting Mark to identify a range of positive qualities he had previously demonstrated to significant others, with an accessible memory associated with each quality. Mark identified positive traits as being 'generous, caring and helpful to others' through recalling the difficult period when he was sole carer for his younger brother and occasionally having to go without food so his brother could enjoy a meal. BMAC practices allowed Mark to repeatedly access these memories and associated feelings, which were followed by reflection with the therapist on what such feelings mean about Mark and the positive relationships he had with his family and friends. Through continued practice, Mark self-reported an increasing confidence in being able to manage his mood by using the range of BMAC practices when he noticed a downward change to his mood. A relapse prevention plan was developed in the final sessions.

Mark completed self-report questionnaire measures at baseline, end of therapy and 6 months follow-up. Mark's score for the probability of potential suicide decreased from the high suicide risk range at baseline to low risk by the end of therapy, which was maintained at follow-up. Similarly, scores for depression and hopelessness fell from the severe range at baseline into the non-clinical range by end of therapy and at follow-up.

Summary

Whilst the prison environment and experience of daily life inside prison can be seriously detrimental to mental health and well-being, the identification of prisoners experiencing mental distress requires improvement. Many prisoners' mental health problems continue to remain both undetected and untreated (Birmingham, 2003). The provision of suitable and effective mental health services to prisoners can be challenging, because the prison environment and regime are not specifically designed to be therapeutic, but rather more focused upon discipline and control (Hughes, 2000; Sim, 1994). Notwithstanding such difficulties, improving the health of prisoners has a number of public health implications. The most important of these is that prisoners are often from marginalised populations that have poor access to healthcare in the community. Because the vast majority of prisoners return to the community, periods of incarceration offer important opportunities for a variety of prevention and treatment interventions, taking advantage of which stands to benefit not only the prisoners themselves, their families, partners and friends, but also the larger public health arena, as well as producing downstream savings in other publicly funded services.

The cognitive behavioural approach to the prevention of suicide has been shown to be an effective intervention for various clinical groups within the community. The extension of this approach to the treatment of suicidal prisoners is feasible. The recent trial of the CBSP therapy demonstrated this approach has the potential to lead to reductions in the incidence of suicidal behaviour by prisoners and significant improvements in established indicators of psychological wellbeing (Pratt et al., in press). Although the first trial of CBSP has provided promising results, the small sample size must encourage caution in the drawing of any firm conclusions at this early stage. Nevertheless, this pilot trial has prepared the way for larger scale trials to confirm these preliminary results.

References

Beck, A. T. (1976). *Cognitive therapy and the emotional disorders.* New York, NY: International Universities Press.

Beck, A. T., & Greenberg, R. L. (1974). *Coping with depression.* New York, NY: Institute for Rational-Emotive Therapy.

Birmingham, L. (2003). The mental health of prisoners. *Advances in Psychiatric Treatment, 9*, 191–201.

Britton, P. C., Williams, G. C., & Conner, K. R. (2008). Self-determination theory, motivational interviewing, and the treatment of clients with acute suicidal ideation. *Journal of Clinical Psychology, 64*(1), 52–66.

Brooker, C., & Gojkovic, D. (2009). The second national survey of mental health in-reach services in prisons. *Journal of Forensic Psychiatry and Psychology, 20* (Sup 1), S11–S28.

Brown, G. K., Ten Have, T. R., Henriques, G. R., Xie, S. X., Hollander, J. E., & Beck, A. T. (2005). Cognitive therapy for the prevention of suicide attempts: A randomized controlled trial. *Journal of the American Medical Association, 294*, 563–570.

Crawford, M. J., Thomas, O., Khan, N., & Kulinskaya, E. (2007). Psychosocial interventions following self-harm: Systematic review of their efficacy in preventing suicide. *British Journal of Psychiatry, 190*, 11–17.

Daigle, M. S., Daniel, A. E., Dear G. E., Frottier, P., Hayes, L. M., Kerkhof, A., . . . Sarchiapone, M. (2007). Preventing suicide in prisons, part II: International comparisons of suicide prevention services in correctional facilities. *Crisis, 28*, 122–130.

Department of Health. (2009). *Improving access to psychological therapies: Offenders – positive practice guide*. London, UK: Author.

66   *Daniel Pratt*

Department of Health and HM Prison Service. (2002). *Developing and modernising primary care in prisons.* London, UK: Department of Health.

Dimidjian, S., Hollon, S.D., Dobson, K.S., Schmaling, K.B., Kohlenberg, R.J., Addis, M.E., . . . and Jacobson, N.S. (2006). Randomized trial of behavioral activation, cognitive therapy, and antidepressant medication in the acute treatment of adults with major depression. *Journal of Consulting and Clinical Psychology, 74*(4), 658–670.

Fredrickson, B.L., & Branigan, C.A. (2005). Positive emotions broaden the scope of attention and thought–action repertoires. *Cognition and Emotion, 19*, 313–332.

Gaynes, B.N., West, S.L., Ford, C.A., Frame, P., Klein, J., & Lohr, K.N. (2004). Screening for suicide risk in adults: A summary of the evidence for the US Preventive Services Task Force. *Annals of Internal Medicine, 140*, 822–835.

Gendreau, P. (1996). The principles of effective intervention with offenders. In A.T. Harland (Ed.), *Choosing correctional options that work: Defining the demand and evaluating the supply* (pp. 117–130). Thousand Oaks, CA: Sage Publications.

Ghahramanlou-Holloway, M., Bhar, S.S., Brown, G.K., Olsen, C., & Beck, A.T. (2012). Changes in problem-solving appraisal after cognitive therapy for the prevention of suicide. *Psychological Medicine, 42*, 1185–1193.

Hanson, A. (2010). Correctional suicide: Has progress ended? *Journal of the American Academy of Psychiatry and the Law, 38*, 6–10.

Harvey, J. (2007). *Young men in prison: Surviving and adapting to life inside.* Cullompton, Devon, UK: Willan Publishing.

Harvey, J. (2011). Acknowledging and understanding complexity when providing therapy in prisons. *European Journal of Psychotherapy and Counselling, 13*, 303–315.

Hayes, L.M. (2010). Toward a better understanding of suicide prevention in correctional facilities. In C.L. Scott (Ed.), *Handbook of correctional mental health* (pp. 231–254). Arlington, VA: American Psychiatric Publishing.

HM Prison Service. (2005). *PSI 18/2005: Introducing ACCT (Assessment, Care in Custody and Teamwork) – the replacement for the F2052SH (Risk of Self-Harm).* London, UK: Author.

Hughes, R. (2000). Health, place and British prisons. *Health and Place, 6*, 57–62.

International Association for Correctional and Forensic Psychology Practice Standards Committee. (2010). Standards for psychology services in jails, prisons, correctional facilities, and agencies. *Criminal Justice and Behavior, 37*, 749–808.

Jacobson, N.S., Martell, C.R., & Dimidjian, S. (2001). Behavioral activation treatment for depression: Returning to contextual roots. *Clinical Psychology: Science and Practice, 8*(3), 255–270.

Johnson, J., Gooding, P., & Tarrier, N. (2008). Suicide risk in schizophrenia: Explanatory models and clinical implications, The Schematic Appraisal Model of Suicide (SAMS). *Psychology and Psychotherapy: Theory, Research and Practice, 81*, 55–77.

Konrad, N., Daigle, M.S., Daniel, A.E., Dear, G.E., Frottier, P., Hayes, L.M., . . . Sarchiapone, M. (2007). Preventing suicide in prisons, part I: Recommendations from the International Association for Suicide Prevention task force on suicide in prisons. *Crisis, 28*, 113–121.

Liebling, A., Durie, L., Stiles, A., & Tait, S. (2005). Revisiting prison suicide: The role of fairness and distress. In A. Liebling & S. Maruna (Eds.), *The effects of imprisonment* (pp. 209–231). Cullompton, Devon, UK: Willan Publishing.

Liebling, A., & Maruna, S. (2005). *The effects of imprisonment.* Cullompton, Devon, UK: Willan Publishing.

Lipsey, M. W., Landenberger, N. A., & Wilson, S. J. (2007). Effects of cognitive behavioural programs for criminal offenders. *Campbell Systematic Reviews, 6,* 1–27.

Mann, J. J., Apter, A., Bertolote, J., Beautrais, A., Currier, D., Haas, A., . . . Hendin, H. (2005). Suicide prevention strategies: A systematic review. *Journal of the American Medical Association, 294,* 2064–2074.

McDougall, C., Perry, A. E., Clarbour, J., Bowles, R., & Worthy, G. (2009). *Evaluation of HM prison service enhanced thinking skills programme: Report on the outcomes from a randomised controlled trial (Ministry of Justice Research Series 3/09).* London, UK: Ministry of Justice.

McGuire, J. (Ed.). (2002). *Offender rehabilitation and treatment: Effective programmes and policies to reduce re-offending.* Chichester, UK: Wiley.

Ministry of Justice. (2011). *Safety in Custody 2010: England and Wales.* London, UK: Author.

Murray, J. (2007). The cycle of punishment: Social exclusion of prisoners and their children. *Criminology and Criminal Justice, 7,* 55–81.

Panagioti, M., Gooding, P., Taylor, P., & Tarrier, N. (2012). Negative self-appraisals and suicidal behavior among trauma victims experiencing PTSD symptoms: the mediating role of defeat and entrapment. *Depression and Anxiety, 29*(3), 187–194.

Pollock, L. R., & Williams, J.M.G. (1998). Problem solving and suicidal behavior. *Suicide and Life-Threatening Behavior, 28*(4), 375–387.

Pompili, M., Lester, D., Innamorati, M., Del Casale, A., Girardi, P., Ferracuti, S., & Tatarelli, R. (2009). Preventing suicide in jails and prisons: Suggestions from experience with psychiatric inpatients. *Journal of Forensic Sciences, 54,* 1155–1162.

Pratt, D., Tarrier, N., Dunn, G., Awenat, Y., Shaw, J., Ulph, F., & Gooding, P. (in press). Cognitive behavioural suicide prevention for male prisoners: A pilot randomised controlled trial. *Psychological Medicine.*

Sim, J. (1994). Prison medicine and social justice. *Prison Service Journal, 95,* 30–38.

Slee, N., Garnefski, N., van der Leeden, R., Arensman, E., & Spinhoven, P. (2008). Cognitive–behavioural intervention for self-harm: Randomised controlled trial. *British Journal of Psychiatry, 192*(3), 202–211.

Social Exclusion Unit. (2002). *Reducing re-offending by ex-prisoners.* London, UK: Author.

Tarrier, N. (2010). Broad Minded Affective Coping (BMAC): A "positive" CBT approach to facilitating positive emotions. *International Journal of Cognitive Therapy, 3,* 64–76.

Tarrier, N., Gooding, P., Pratt, D., Kelly, J., Awenat, Y., & Maxwell, J. (2013). *Cognitive behavioural prevention of suicide in psychosis: A treatment manual.* London, UK: Routledge.

Tarrier, N., Kelly, J., Maqsood, S., Snelson, N., Maxwell, J., Law, H., . . . Gooding, P. (2014). The cognitive behavioural prevention of suicide in psychosis: A clinical trial. *Schizophrenia Research, 156*(2), 204–210.

Tarrier, N., Taylor, K., & Gooding, P. (2008). Cognitive-behavioral interventions to reduce suicide behavior: A systematic review and meta-analysis. *Behavior Modification, 32*, 77–108.

Taylor, P.J., Gooding, P.A., Wood, A.M., Johnson, J., Pratt, D., & Tarrier, N. (2010). Defeat and entrapment in schizophrenia: The relationship with suicidal ideation and positive psychotic symptoms. *Psychiatry Research, 178*(2), 244–248.

US Department of Health and Human Services. (2001). National strategy for suicide prevention: Goals and objectives for action. Rockville, MD: Public Health Service.

Wells, A. (2009). *Metacognitive therapy for anxiety and depression*. London, UK: Guilford Press.

Wenzel, A., Brown, G.K., & Beck, A.T. (2009). *Cognitive therapy for suicidal patients: Scientific and clinical applications*. Washington, DC: American Psychological Association.

Williams, C., & Garland, A. (2002). A cognitive–behavioural therapy assessment model for use in everyday clinical practice. *Advances in Psychiatric Treatment, 8*(3), 172–179.

Williams, J.M.G., & Pollock, L.R. (2000). The psychology of suicidal behaviour. In K. Hawton & K. van Heeringen (Eds.), *The international handbook of suicide and attempted suicide* (pp 79–93). Chichester, UK: Wiley.

World Health Organization. (2008). *Trenčin statement on prisons and mental health*. Copenhagen, Denmark: Author.

5 Problem-solving training for suicidal prisoners

Amanda Perry, Mitch Waterman and Allan House

Introduction

Self-harm has been a major health problem in the UK for 50 years. Rates have never been collected for England nationally, but estimates based on Department of Health–funded multi-centre monitoring (Manchester, Oxford and Derby) suggest that rates in hospital presentations included around 350 males and 480 females per 100,000 per annum (Bergen, Hawton, Waters, Cooper, & Kapur, 2010). However, many of those who self-harm are based in prisons (and do not therefore attend hospital), and rates of self-harm and eventual suicide far exceed the rate within the general population (Fazel, Grann, Kling, & Hawton, 2011). A recent case control prison study estimated that the annual prevalence of self-harm in custody was between 5–6% for men and teenage boys and 20–24% in women and adolescent girls (Hawton, Linsell, Adeniji, Sariaslan, & Fazel, 2014). This proportion is much higher than the 0.6% of the UK general population who reported self-harm in the preceding year (Bebbington, Minot, & Cooper, 2010). In addition, self-harm is a major problem in the prison environment because individuals often repeatedly harm themselves, and such repetition has been shown to increase the probable risk of ultimate suicide. Eventual suicides are 5 times higher in male prisoners and 20 times higher in female inmates than in general population controls (Fazel & Benning, 2009; Fazel, Benning, & Danesh, 2005). As many as 1.8% of people who harm themselves die by suicide in the year following the incident (Owens, Horrocks, & House, 2002), and in the community as many as 8.5% die by suicide over a 22-year-period (Jenkins, McCulloch, & Friedli, 2002).

Treatment of self-harm behaviour in prisons is generally anecdotal but has been improved in recent years through several initiatives, including the introduction of Safer Custody measures through the Assessment, Care in Custody and Teamwork (ACCT) system (UK Ministry of Justice, 2013), enhanced mental health services and piecemeal environmental improvements (Forrester & Slade, 2014). Despite these improvements, a renewed approach to the care of prisoners who self-harm is required alongside the need for raising staff awareness and further training as important issues in the prevention of self-harm and suicide in prisoners (Hawton et al., 2014).

Possible treatment options are unclear from the evidence for a number of reasons. First, a handful of trials have been conducted in the community with individuals who self-harm but not with offender populations. Second, data particularly on repetition of self-harm have been limited in previous trials (Hawton et al., 2000). However, one potential treatment that shows promising results for the repetition of self-harm behaviour is problem-solving therapy (PST). This is particularly useful because evidence from experimental studies suggests that studies of patients who have attempted suicide have shown specific deficits in problem-solving abilities (e.g., Linehan, Camper, Chiles, Strosahl, & Shearin, 1987; Schotte & Clum, 1987), consistent with the hypothesis that attempted suicide may relate to failures of problem solving at times of crisis.

Poor problem-solving skills are associated with impulsive responding and incomplete solutions. With people who have self-harmed, they display less active problem solving, reliance on the actions of others, waiting for resolution, and poor generation of alternative solutions. The first and most obvious reason to offer PST is because so many people who harm themselves report the main immediate cause as being problems in their lives. Research also suggests that people who attempt suicide can have poor problem-solving skills more generally (Linehan et al., 1987; McLeavey, Daly, Murray, O'Riordan, Taylor, 1987; Pollock & Williams, 2001). Typically, they tend to be less active in their problem-solving efforts. Many rely on the actions of others or the passage of time to solve the problem rather than taking an active part in solving the problem (Pollock & Williams, 2001).

Social problem solving stems from a concept originally outlined by Skinner (Skinner, 1953) and Davis (Davis, 1966) whereby the approach of problem solving is defined as a self-directed cognitive behavioural process by which a person attempts to identify or discover effective or adaptive ways of coping with problematic situations. The role of coping within problem solving has been recognised as using two different information processing systems that play a role: an automatic or experiential system and a non-automatic or rational system, which includes rational problem solving. The automatic response is a result of rapid decision making and is intuitively validated as 'feeling right'. The non-automatic or rational system is a slower process whereby deliberate and logical decisions are made most likely when critical problematic situations arise where 'much is at stake' and the automatic retrieval process has failed to produce any adequate or acceptable solution.

This research is supported by D'Zurilla and colleagues (1998), who noted that individuals who are "suicide prone" have a characteristic set of negative thoughts and feelings about problems and about their ability to solve problems. Typically, they perceive problems as some sort of a threat to their well-being. They tend to blame themselves for problems when they occur and doubt their own ability to solve problems effectively. They are more likely to view problems as unsolvable and to feel distressed and upset when faced with a problem. D'Zurilla and colleagues (1998) go on to suggest that these beliefs and feelings have an impact on how people actually respond to problems. Instead of facing problems as they arise, and being persistent in their problem-solving efforts, the suicide-prone individual is likely to either avoid problems or respond impulsively. When avoiding problems, he or she tends to either put off solving problems for as long as possible, wait for problems to resolve themselves or try to shift the responsibility for solving problems on to others. When responding impulsively, the person does attempt to solve problems, but these attempts are not well thought out. Avoidant and impulsive responses are not likely to result in effective problem solving and thus risk reinforcing the negative beliefs and feelings (D'Zurilla & Goldfried, 1971).

Original experimental studies conducted first in 1978 and later in the 1990s have developed a growing body of evidence to support the use of PST with patients who self-harm or who are at risk of suicide. Individual trial data have shown a variety of results, with some moderate improvements in problem-solving skills, depression, hopelessness and self-harm repetition. The most recent research has used meta-analytical techniques to combine trial data to provide an overall effect for different types of outcomes. Two systematic reviews provide tentative support for the use of problem-solving techniques (Hawton et al., 2009; Townsend et al., 2001). The first of these combine two of six randomised controlled trials (RCTs) for the treatment of deliberate self- harm behaviour (containing a total of 71 and 55 individuals assigned to the intervention and control groups).

The results overall showed that patients who were offered the therapy had significantly greater improvement in scores for depression and hopelessness and also importantly reported a greater level of improvement in their problems in comparison with those in the control group. One of the two trials showed a non-significant result (Gibbons, Butler, Urwin, & Gibbons, 1978), and the other showed a clear significant reduction in the numbers of problems reported; together they produced an overall reduction

(Hawton et al., 1987). However, concerns with regards to trial size have been reported by other researchers (US Preventive Services Task Force, 2004), which judged the existing studies to have three main limitations: a lack of power, poor description of standard care and inconsistent age ranges across studies (Cooper et al., 2005).

The second review found similar findings. Hawton et al. (2000), as part of a larger Cochrane systematic review focusing on psychological therapies for self-harm, included trials comparing problem solving interventions alongside standard treatment. The problem solving meta-analysis showed a trend towards ($OR = 0.70$; 95% CI 0.45 to 1.11) reduced repetition of self-harm for problem solving therapy compared with standard aftercare (Evans et al., 1999; Gibbons et al., 1978; Hawton et al., 1987; McLeavey, Daly, Ludgate, & Murray, 1994; Salkovskis, Atha, & Storer, 1990). Since this 2009 review, we sought to identify any further trials using PST. We identified two further trials of PST in patients that self-harmed. Figure 5.1 shows the existing problem-solving trials identified by Hawton and colleagues combined with the results of the two most recent trials (Hatcher, Sharon, Parag, & Collins, 2011; Morthorst, Krogh, Erlangsen, Alberdi, & Nordentoft, 2012). The addition of the two new trials on outcomes of repetition show modest effects in favour of PST for repetition of self-harm ($OR = 0.70$; 95% CI 0. 45–1.10).

The first of these two trials evaluated the effect of PST in adults presenting to hospital following self-harm (defined as intentional self-poisoning or self-injury, irrespective of motivation). Patients were randomised to PST plus usual care or usual care alone. PST consisted of at least 4, and up to 9, sessions (including problem orientation, problem listing and definition, brainstorming and devising an action plan) starting as soon as possible after the index episode and lasting for up to 3 months. Follow up-data on hospital presentations were obtained for 100% of randomised patients. The primary outcome was presentation to hospital following self-harm in the 12 months subsequent to the index presentation (Hatcher et al., 2011).

An intention-to-treat analysis among patients whose index episode was their first presentation for self-harm showed no significant difference in the proportion of repeat self-harm between the groups ($p = 0.37$). However, for those initially presenting with repeat self-harm, PST was associated with significantly less re-presentation at 12 months ($RR = 0.39$, 95% CI 0.07 to 0.60, $p = 0.03$). Among this sub-group, there was also a significantly shorter time to repetition of self-harm (hazard ratio [HR] = 0.58, 95% CI 0.36 to 0.94, $p = 0.03$) than usual care. Participants who received PST also had significantly greater changes in outcomes of hopelessness, depression and anxiety.

Study or subgroup	Problem solving		Care as usual		Weight	Odds ratio M-H, Random, 95% CI	Odds ratio M-H, Random, 95% CI
	Events	Total	Events	Total			
Salkovskis, 1990	3	12	4	8	5.0%	0.33 [0.05, 2.24]	
McLeavy, 1994	2	19	5	20	5.6%	0.35 [0.06, 2.09]	
Hawton, 1987	3	41	6	39	7.9%	0.43 [0.10, 1.87]	
Hatcher, 2011	26	88	49	104	25.9%	0.47 [0.26, 0.86]	
Evans, 1999	10	18	10	14	7.7%	0.50 [0.11, 2.21]	
Gibbons, 1978	27	200	29	200	27.2%	0.92 [0.52, 1.62]	
Morthorst, 2012	20	123	13	120	20.6%	1.60 [0.76, 3.38]	
Total (95%CI)		501		505	100.0%	0.70 [0.45, 1.10]	
Total events	91		116				

Heterogeneity: Tau² = 0.11; Chi² = 8.94, df = 6 (P = 0.18); I² = 33%
Test for overall effect: Z = 1.54 (P = 0.12)

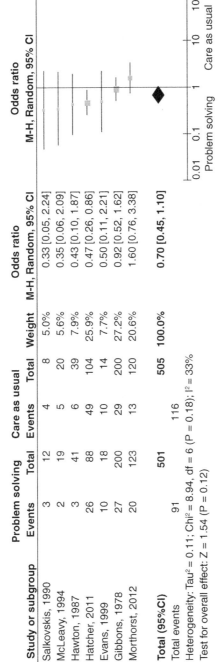

Figure 5.1 Forest plot of problem-solving interventions on repetition of self-harm

One potential limitation of the study related to the Zelen design of asking for consent after randomisation. This introduced the possibility of selection bias as those who consented to the two arms may have differed from one another in some way. However, in this trial, those consenting to problem solving had poorer prognostic markers at baseline than those consenting to usual care, which may add weight to the significant differences observed. The data suggest that although PST appeared to be no more effective than usual care in preventing repetition of self-harm among people presenting with self-harm for the first time, for those presenting with recurrent self-harm it may be more effective than standard care (Hatcher et al., 2011).

The second of the two trials evaluated an assertive outreach intervention following a suicide attempt. Patients were randomised to standard treatment or to the 'assertive intervention for deliberate self-harm' (AID) intervention. Standard treatment consisted of referral to relevant treatments following psychiatric evaluation (such as psychotherapy or treatment for alcohol abuse). The AID intervention involved case management with crisis intervention, problem solving, assertive outreach through motivational support and assisting participants to and from appointments to improve compliance. Data for repeated suicide attempts and death by suicide were recovered from hospital registration, medical records and self-reported data (Morthorst et al., 2012).

During a one-year follow-up, there was no difference in the number of suicide attempts between the AID and the standard care groups on the basis of either hospital records (20/123 vs. 13/120 respectively; $OR = 1.60$, 95% CI 0.76 to 3.38, $p = 0.22$) or self-reported data (11/95 vs. 13/74 respectively; $OR = 0.61$, 95% CI 0.26 to 1.46, $p = 0.27$). Analyses following imputation of missing data for the self-reported outcomes, or combining hospital with self-reported data, did not significantly alter results. Limitations of the evidence included

1   The treatment available to those in the control group, which could potentially have lessened the relative impact of the AID intervention (although qualifying participants from both groups were able to access these sessions);
2   Differing levels of baseline anti-depressant use between groups may have been a source of bias (although adjustment for this did not indicate any);
3   The study may not have been powered to detect the smaller differences between groups present in the trial; and
4   Between hospital and self-reported data, which may have been a result of under-estimation or over-estimation of suicide attempts in self-reports.

Although the trials remain small in numbers, the results in Figure 5.1 (representing now seven trials with a total of 501 intervention and 555 control participants) show a trend towards favouring the use of problem solving for *repetition* of self-harm behaviour. Whilst this collection of trials provide a basis for future use of this therapy in the community, use of PST for treatment of self-harm in the prison environment, remains untested. To address this gap in the literature, we describe the methodology of a new study of PST for offenders of repeat self-harm behaviour in four different prison settings across the UK.

Feasibility of implementing problem solving in prisons

The principal aim of the study is to develop a problem-solving intervention to reduce self-harm in prisons. The intervention has two components: a training programme, the aim of which is to equip all wing staff in the prison with a basic understanding of the problem-solving approach, and a further, more detailed training for staff who deal with prisoners considered at risk of self-harm or suicide, to assist them in delivering a more prisoner-centred support for prisoners so identified. The study will take place in four prisons across the UK, and the findings will be used to determine the feasibility of a large-scale evaluation of the intervention. The study has a number of objectives:

1   An assessment of the feasibility and acceptability of the problem-solving intervention, using qualitative methods;
2   An assessment of the feasibility of undertaking an evaluation of the intervention using changes in prison behaviour as judged by routinely collected data and involving a quasi-experimental (interrupted time series) design;
3   An assessment of the feasibility of collecting individual outcomes for those prisoners who were identified as being at risk of self-harm or suicide and received additional support from staff trained in problem-solving techniques as part of the project;
4   To follow prisoners on release to assess any further utilization of healthcare resources.

Four prisons in the North of England will provide a representative sample of staff and patients for inclusion in the study. For the staff training, the project team will invite all staff within each prison to participate, including management, probation, teaching and prison officers, chaplaincy, psychologists, specialist suicide prevention assessors and nursing staff. Data will be collected about the characteristics of staff that do and do not complete the training to explore the reasons behind non-compliance with the program.

For the specialist intervention with at-risk prisoners, we will invite every patient under the care of the ACCT system while the intervention is being implemented. The ACCT system is currently used by all staff to provide a mechanism for monitoring and developing an individualised care plan with an individual who is thought to be at risk of self-harm behavior, suicidal or both. ACCT is prisoner centred and covers a number of stages that must be conducted within specific timescales. The ethos of the ACCT system focuses on the responsibility of all staff to identify and manage prisoners at risk of suicide, self-harm or both. Prison documentation notes that good staff/prisoner relationships are integral to reducing risk, and participation in regime activities, positive family and peer relationships and referral to appropriate specialist services such as mental health in reach, play a role.

The intervention

The intervention will be delivered and disseminated throughout each prison using two training phases and an implementation phase. Phase one will involve the delivery of a generic problem-solving intervention (Package A) to all staff, through a trained mental health facilitator. The mental health facilitator will have training in teaching methods and education in all skills and knowledge included in the training package. The generic staff training consists of two modular standalone training sessions each up to one hour in length. The first session will include an interactive skills-based session teaching the principles of problem-solving skills and containing a mixture of learning options, including group, individual and self-guided learning based on examples while at work. Between sessions, staff will be encouraged to use their new skills and provide a portfolio of examples for discussion in session two. Staff will be trained in groups of up to eight members. It is intended that this training would be sustained as part of the staff induction process once the research is complete. It will be assumed that all staff will have limited previous mental health training, and as such our intervention will be aimed at those with no prior knowledge or experience. This will ensure that all levels of staff experience will be considered.

Phase two will deliver a tailor-made specific intervention (Package B) to staff who are trained to deal specifically with prisoners at risk (suicide prevention coordinators and nursing staff). In the implementation phase, staff will use the skills they have learnt with patients at risk, over a two-month period in each prison. Specific problem-solving skills for suicide prevention co-ordinators and nursing staff will last up to one hour. The training will be taught in small groups or on an individual basis, dependent upon the availability of staff working arrangements. The session will focus on (i) improving the ability of staff to identify problem-solving deficits, (ii) promoting coping strategies, and (iii) assessing triggers for risk of self-harm. The session will involve a series of role plays with actors playing the part of prisoners. Although paid actors will be used, the feasibility of using other prisoners (currently trained through the Listener scheme to help patients in crisis) will be explored as a way of involving patients in the development of the package. For example we will consult with prisoners on the development of the training materials, consent forms and information sheets to ensure that they are appropriate for use.

Suicide prevention coordinators and nursing staff will implement the intervention with individuals identified at risk under the ACCT system. This single 30-minute session will ensure that the total intervention will be received by patients even if they transferred or released shortly afterwards. The session will take place shortly after the first assessment using the ACCT system. Subsequent ACCT meetings will include a repeated 15-minute session with the patient until the ACCT system is no longer required to support the patient. This model will minimise attrition and allow us to assess different levels of dosage and intensity of the intervention delivered by staff. Patients will be given worksheets that will help them think about their thoughts, feelings and actions prior to an incident of self-harm behaviour. The worksheets and reinforcement of help-seeking skills will form part of the care plan for the individual and will be subsequently followed until no further support is required. Evidence of treatment fidelity will be monitored by evidenced documentation, including reflection sheets and solution implementation.

A case study example

PST involves a number of stages starting with problem orientation, followed by recognising and identifying problems, selecting and defining a clear problem-generating solution, decision making, creating and implementing an action plan and the process of reviewing progress. Throughout the training, examples of case studies are used to demonstrate the different possibilities of PST in action within a forensic setting.

Introducing James

> The following case study, James, is unfortunately typical of many young men who end up in prison with a number of life problems and a series of risk factors linked to his self-harm behaviour. James is suddenly faced with a crisis that he finds particularly frustrating and difficult to cope with.

James is a 22-year-old man with a partner of one year. He has two children via previous relationships and a 6-month-old baby with his current partner. James is one of six siblings born to his father and stepmother. James's relationship with his parents was troubled from a young age, and his father would come home and beat James when drunk. His stepmother found it difficult to deal with his aggressive emotional outbursts, and James was excluded from school at age 11 for poor behaviour and emotional outbursts. He started to mix with a gang of older boys who were known in the area for committing petty crimes. James became involved in drugs at age 13 years and was caught by the police for burglary when he was 16 years old. He also had a series of relationships with older women, which led to a number of pregnancies resulting in two sons. James's stepmother was unable to control his behaviour and did not want him in the house anymore, so James was asked to leave. James went at first to stay with a friend but soon moved to a hostel. James found it difficult to get a job and quickly used crime to support his drug habit. His physical and mental health deteriorated dramatically and he no longer took care of his personal appearance. One day he took a concoction of drugs and alcohol, causing him to overdose, and leading to admission to Accident and Emergency. James was finally convicted for a series of burglaries and was sentenced to prison for the first time age 19 years. At an all-time low, James had no contact with his family and regularly self-harmed when he was feeling particularly stressed. In prison, James was placed in a shared cell and initially in a safe cell. Having settled into prison life, James felt angry and frustrated.

On a recent family prison visit James's partner told him that the council were planning to change their accommodation because he was no longer living with them in the house. The change in circumstances would mean that they may be moved outside of the local area.

James returned to the wing in a low mood, feeling inadequate and powerless to do anything about the change in circumstances. James 'kicks off' in his cell, and when wing staff intervene he blurts out his problem to his key officer.

Recognising and identifying problems

The training package begins with an introduction to the idea of recognising problems and trigger factors; the process of problem solving involves getting the client to identify thoughts, behaviours, feelings and physical symptoms associated with their particular problem. Selecting and defining a problem is helpful in turning ill-defined problems such as 'my life is a mess' into a well-defined problem that the client has control over. In James's case, the problem is clearly defined. The next step is to generate a range of possible solutions.

Generating solutions

Facilitators are asked to work with a client to discuss what possible options are available to resolve or improve the situation. Brainstorming is a method of generating as many possibilities and alternative solutions to the problem without evaluating the potential usefulness. We re-join James at the point at which he is attempting to brainstorm his options and think of alternative ways to resolve his problem.

James felt daunted by trying out brainstorming. At first, he felt that nothing would help the situation. As James and his prison officer started to work together, he gained momentum with the situation and provided a number of different ideas that helped him feel more in control of the situation.

Problem: "My partner is being forced to move out of her house and is being moved away from the area, and I will not see my family every week at visiting time."

- Ask my partner to ring the council and find out where she is moving to
- Arrange a specific time when they will be able to visit so I can look forward to the visit
- Get some photos of my baby and partner to put up in my cell
- Ring my partner more often
- Talk to prison staff to see if I can get extended visiting time when they come
- Focus on keeping myself to myself and not getting into trouble whilst in prison
- Plan the time I have in prison to keep me busy

- Ask if I can have extra jobs to do in the prison to keep my mind occupied
- Go to the prison gym and take part in some exercise
- Consider going to education to see if they have any courses I can attend

Decision making

Once the client has identified a number of potential solutions, the next step is decision making. In this stage, a more in-depth examination of the solutions allows the individual to weigh the advantages and disadvantages of potential solutions. We see James grouping his actions into different categories, ready to choose a final solution and develop an action plan.

When James looked at the initial selection to his brainstorm he decided to cross out several of the options. He thought they lacked feasibility and would have a negative effect on his well-being. Then, James grouped the remaining ideas into three categories:

- Activities to keep him busy
- Methods of organising time
- Strategies to manage stress

After thinking about the advantages and disadvantages of these possibilities, James decided that planning time in advance had the advantage of reducing his stress. James's solution was first to speak to his personnel officer about contacting education and the jobs section within the prison to find out more about what opportunities were available to him. He thought there might be opportunities to keep him busy and organise his time. James also wanted to ring his partner to discuss the move location and ask her to send some pictures of the baby for his cell wall. He thought this would help with the stress and help keep his family in mind, even if he couldn't see them so often. Overall, James thought the combination of these two strategies had a good chance of allowing him to feel better about his time in prison and seeing his family less.

Creating a SMART action plan

The final stages of problem solving involve the client implementing or carrying out an action plan. This should be a step-by-step process that is used to transform the chosen solutions into concrete actions. A SMART (Specific, Measurable, Achievable, Relevant, Time-bound) plan that is focused around when, where, whom and how is key to a successful plan. Identifying barriers to solving the problem needs to be addressed when the plan was not successfully carried out or did not solve the problem. As a facilitator, the important elements of the process also involve reviewing progress with the client to evaluate whether the plan is underway, whether it is having the desired impact, whether any more needs to be done in relation to the problem and to understand the key areas which may need to be fine-tuned.

Summary

In summary, PST has been employed with a number of different community samples with some modest benefits, in particular with those who repeat self-harm. Although these trials show promising results, they are generally small in sample size and do not address the prisoner population. Despite the rate of self-harm being very high in the prison environment, little treatment has been provided to help people cope better with their problems. Repetition in the prison environment is a particular problem and, therefore, PST could provide some support to those who require some help. Our feasibility study will trial the use of PST in the environment, and the study will hopefully lead to the first large-scale trial in the UK of treatment for offenders who self-harm in prison. Lessons about the feasibility of the program and implementation of PST in this environment will help to pave the way for future research and its adaptation into the prison environment.

References

Bebbington, P., Minot, S., & Cooper, C.E.A. (2010). *European Psychiatry, 25*, 427–431.

Bergen, H., Hawton, K., Waters, K., Cooper, J, & Kapur, N. (2010). Epidemiology and trends in non-fatal self-harm in three centres in England, 2000 to 200. *British Journal of Psychiatry, 197*, 493–498.

Cooper, J., Kapur, N., Webb, R., Lawlor, M., Guthrie, E., Mackway-Jones, K., & Appleby, L. (2005). Suicide after deliberate self-harm: A 4-year cohort study. *American Journal of Psychiatry, 162*(2), 297–303. doi:10.1176/appi.ajp.162.2.297

Davis, G.A. (1966). Current status of research and theory in human problem solving. *Psychological Bulletin, 66*(1), 36–54.

D'Zurilla, T.J., Chang, E.C., Nottingham, E.J., & Faccini, L. (1998). Social problem-solving deficits and hopelessness, depression, and suicidal risk in college students and psychiatric inpatients. *Journal of Clinical Psychology, 54*, 1091–1107.

D'Zurilla, T.J., & Goldfried, M.R. (1971). Problem solving and behavior modification. *Journal of Abnormal Psychology, 78*(1), 107–126.

Evans, K., Tyrer, P., Catalan, J., Schmidt, U., Davidson, K., Dent, J., . . . Thompson, S. (1999). Manual assisted cognitive behavioural therapy in the treatment of recurrent deliberate self harm: A randomised controlled trial. *Psychological Medicine, 29*, 19–25.

Fazel, S., & Benning, R. (2009). Suicides in female prisoners in England and Wales, 1978–2004. *British Journal of Psychiatry, 194*(2), 183–184. doi:10.1192/bjp.bp.107.046490

Fazel, S., Benning, R., & Danesh, J. (2005). Suicides in male prisoners in England and Wales, 1978–2003. *Lancet, 366*(9493), 1301–1302. doi:10.1016/S0140-6736(05)67325-4

Fazel, S., Grann, M., Kling, B., & Hawton, K. (2011). Prison suicide in 12 countries: An ecological study of 861 suicides during 2003–2007. *Social Psychiatry and Psychiatric Epidemiology, 46*(3), 191–195. doi:10.1007/s00127-010-0184-4

Forrester, A., & Slade, K. (2014). Preventing self-harm and suicide in prisoners: Job half done. *Lancet, 383*(9923), 1109–1111. Doi:10.1016/S0140-6736(13)62571-4

Gibbons, J.S., Butler, J., Urwin, P., & Gibbons, J.L. (1978). Evaluation of a social work service for self-poisoning patients. *British Journal of Psychiatry, 133*(2), 111–118. doi:10.1192/bjp.133.2.111

Hatcher, S., Sharon, C., Parag, V., & Collins, N. (2011). Problem-solving therapy for people who present to hospital with self-harm: Zelen randomised controlled trial. *British Journal of Psychiatry, 199*(4), 310–316. doi:10.1192/bjp.bp.110.090126

Hawton, K., Linsell, L., Adeniji, T., Sariaslan, A., & Fazel, S. (2014). Self-harm in prisons in England and Wales: An epidemiological study of prevalence, risk factors, clustering, and subsequent suicide. *Lancet, 383*(9923), 1147–1154. doi:10.1016/S0140-6736(13)62118-2

Hawton, K., McKeown, S., Day, A., Martin, P., O'Connor, M., & Yule, J. (1987). Evaluation of out-patient counselling compared with general practitioner care following overdoses. *Psychological Medicine, 17*(3), 751–761.

Hawton, K., Townsend, E., Arensman, E., Gunnell, D., Hazell, P., House, A., & van Heeringen, K. (2000). Psychosocial and pharmacological treatments for deliberate self harm. *Cochrane Depression, Anxiety and Neurosis Group.* doi:10.1002/14651858.CD001764

Jenkins, R., McCulloch, A., Friedli, L., & Parker, C. (2002). Developing a National Mental Health Policy. Maudsley Monographs no. 43. Hove, UK: Psychology Press.

Linehan, M.M., Camper, P., Chiles, J.A., Strosahl, K., & Shearin, E. (1987). Interpersonal problem-solving and parasuicide. *Cognitive Therapy and Research, 11*(1), 1–12. doi:10.1007/Bf01183128

McLeavey, B.C., Daly, R.J., Murray, C.M., O'Riordan, J., & Taylor, M. (1987). Interpersonal problem-solving deficits in self-poisoning patients. *Suicide and Life-Threatening Behavior, 17*, 33–49.

McLeavey, B.C., Daly, R.J., Ludgate, J.W., & Murray, C.M. (1994). Interpersonal problem-solving skills training in the treatment of self-poisoning patients. *Suicide and Life-Threatening Behavior,* 24(4), 382–394. doi:10.1111/j.1943-278X.1994. tb00817.x

Morthorst, B., Krogh, J., Erlangsen, A., Alberdi, F., & Nordentoft, M. (2012). Effect of assertive outreach after suicide attempt in the AID (assertive intervention for deliberate self harm) trial: Randomised controlled trial. *British Medical Journal, 345,* e4972. doi:10.1136/bmj.e4972

Owens, D., Horrocks, J., & House, A. (2002). Fatal and non-fatal repetition of self-harm. Systematic review. *British Journal of Psychiatry, 181*(3), 193–199. doi:10.1192/bjp.181.3.193

Pollock, L.R., & Williams, J.M.G. (2001). Effective problem solving in suicide attempters depends on specific autobiographical recall. *Suicide and Life-Threatening Behavior, 31,* 386–396.

Salkovskis, P.M., Atha, C., & Storer, D. (1990). Cognitive-behavioural problem solving in the treatment of patients who repeatedly attempt suicide: A controlled trial. British Journal of Psychiatry, 157(6), 871–876. doi:10.1192/bjp.157.6.871

Schotte, D.E., & Clum, G.A. (1987). Problem solving skills in suicidal psychiatric patients. *Journal of Consulting and Clinical Psychology, 55,* 49–54.

Skinner, B.F. (1953). *Science and human behavior.* New York, NY: Macmillan.

Townsend, E., Hawton, K., Altman, D.G., Arensman, E., Gunnell, D., Hazell, P., . . . Van Heeringen, K. (2001). The efficacy of problem-solving treatments after deliberate self-harm: Meta-analysis of randomized controlled trials with respect to depression, hopelessness and improvement in problems. *Psychological Medicine, 31*(6), 979–988.

UK Ministry of Justice. (2013). *Management of prisoners at risk of harm to self, to others and from others (safer custody).* Retrieved from http://www.justice.gov.uk/ offenders/psis/prison-serviceinstructions-2011

US Preventive Services Task Force. (2004). Screening for suicide risk: Recommendation and rationale. *Annals of Internal Medicine, 140,* 820–821.

6 Forensic patient and public involvement

The development and maintenance of an ex-offender service user reference group

Yvonne Awenat

Background

Patient and Public Involvement (PPI), also termed 'service user involvement', in research is now accepted as highly desirable if not mandatory in order to obtain funding from most national funding bodies (e.g. NIHR). Patient and Public Involvement is defined by INVOLVE (the leading national organization in the UK responsible for PPI within the NHS and statutory social care services) as:

> An active partnership between the public and researchers in the research process. Active involvement may take the form of consultation, collaboration or user control. Many people define public involvement in research as doing research 'with' or 'by' the public rather than 'to' or 'about' or 'for' the public. This would include, for example, public involvement in prioritising research, advising on a research project, assisting in the design of a project, or in carrying out the research.
>
> (INVOLVE, 2014)

Involvement, therefore, is distinct from *participation* in research, where in the latter case the individual is a volunteer within the sample to be studied. The underlying rationale for service user *involvement* in research is that a person with 'lived experience' of a situation, for example a health condition or treatment, is able to offer a 'real-time' perspective on the basis of direct personal experiences viewed through the lens of the recipient. Professionals whose orientation is primarily from a clinical or academic perspective will naturally focus on applying their work-related technical expertise, and any interpretations made of the service user situation will inevitably always be limited by the lack of direct personal experience.

Collectives of service users and carers working in partnership with research teams to provide advice and guidance throughout the course of a research study are commonly termed 'Service User Reference Groups' (SURGs). Whilst SURGs are increasingly becoming accepted as a fairly standard feature within certain fields of research, it remains unusual to find these within forensic health studies. Indeed, to the best of our knowledge, and at the time of writing, the SURG within the Prevention of Suicide in Prisons (PROSPeR) study is thought to be the first and possibly only such group within the UK. The idea of having forensic service user consultants remains novel, and was particularly so in 2009 when the research proposal for the PROSPeR study was in preparation and discussions were being held about the possibility of involving people with lived experience of suicidality during a period of imprisonment. More recently, there has been some interest in exploring the possibilities for forensic service user involvement in monitoring and feedback roles within penal institutions (National Survivor User Network, 2011), but such involvement in research remains sparse.

Spiers, Harvey, and Chivers (2005), in discussing the issue of forensic service user involvement in research, describe custodial and secure forensic settings as 'very specialised, potentially dangerous, and unusual' (p. 214), further describing the populations held to include 'difficult, dangerous, or extremely vulnerable people whose behaviours present a risk to themselves as well as to others' (p. 214), and summarising that 'carrying out research in forensic mental health is therefore particularly challenging and the meaningful involvement of forensic mental health service users in the research process presents similar challenges'(p. 214). Clearly then, this was not going to be an easy study, nor was it going to be easy to engage forensic service users in the research!

A truly meaningful study

Inherent in our aspirations for involving people with lived experience was the desire to design a study that would recognise the 'real-time' situation for the suicidal prisoner. As a feasibility study, it was crucial for the research team to be able to understand the inside world of prison life from the perspective of all stakeholders, including prison staff, but especially so concerning prisoner participants as the intended beneficiaries of the research. We were inspired by the success of Professor Anthony Morrison's Service User Reference Group established at the University of Manchester for a five-year study investigating recovery from psychosis, from which groundbreaking approaches to involving 'experts by experience' in the research process were being advanced. However, despite holding such aspirations, at the time of planning the study we had little idea of how to operationalize the plan of setting up a forensic SURG, as there were no forensic specific precedents available to guide us.

The recruitment process

The search for people with the pre-requisite 'lived experience' of experiencing suicidality whilst in prison custody took us on a challenging, laborious and at times highly frustrating journey! We quickly became proficient in the art of compromise, the first instance being that ideally we would have liked to establish a SURG comprising current prisoners from the host prison setting. A basic premise upon which SURGs exist is that members are able to closely reflect the characteristics of the study participants, so in terms of this study, current experience of imprisonment in the host prison bringing with it *live* knowledge of prison practices and routines through the lens of a prisoner would have been ideal. However, this proved impossible because of a number of practical reasons mostly related to the prison security regulations. The availability and location of a suitable meeting room dictated that serving prisoners would have to be taken from their wing to a different venue, and this would require prison staff to be available to accompany them to and from the meeting. Service User Reference Groups become effective when members develop trust and rapport with each other and with the study staff facilitators, which takes time. It soon became apparent that the fluctuating nature of prison populations involving frequent transfers out of the prison often at short notice would challenge the possibility of having a group of regular attendees. So before we had even considered whether any eligible prisoner would be interested in joining a SURG, it was apparent purely on the basis of practicalities that this would not work. The process of having an idea that had worked in a non-forensic setting, then breaking it down into a series of procedural components in terms of what would be required and how this would be affected by the prison regulations soon became very familiar to us! Ways of working that are simple and straightforward requiring little planning in community settings were found here to be complex and presenting additional challenges when applied to the prison setting. In some cases, usual practices in terms of PPI were not translatable to the prison.

So having established that it would not be possible to have a SURG of current serving prisoners, we decided to look for the next best solution of a group of ex-offenders with past experience of feeling suicidal in prison. Several months of searching for statutory and voluntary organizations likely to have contact with ex-offenders resulted in drawing up a list of local and national bodies (e.g. probation services, UNLOCK charity), who we contacted by e-mail or phone to enquire if they could put us in contact with suitable people. Eventually we had a short list of local organizations that were willing to advertise our information flyer in their newsletter or circulate it to individuals. The flyer simply invited people with past experience of use of mental healthcare in a prison, special hospital or secure unit to contact us by phone or e-mail if they were interested in helping with a research project aiming to improve prison healthcare for people at risk of hurting themselves. This resulted in seven people being invited to a group meeting where further information was given about the study, and those still interested were then seen individually to ascertain their suitability to be involved. This brief informal interview provided an opportunity to give further information about the necessary commitment to regular attendance at meetings, to outline the remuneration available and to assess eligibility in terms of the required 'lived experience' and ability to contribute to discussions in a group setting. It also allowed us to stress that the group would be a 'working group' and would not be a 'therapy group'. We have learnt from other experiences that it is very important to make clear to people at the outset that the group is not a setting within which personal problems and personal agendas can be met. Following this, five people were invited to join the SURG.

Forensic service user consultants and their role

The initial group comprised five people: three females and two males, all of whom had served prison sentences and had encountered suicidality. Most individuals resided fairly locally except for one who found attendance difficult to maintain and ultimately dropped out and was subsequently replaced by another male. All consultants were involved in a range of voluntary work activities helping to support others in drug and alcohol recovery, homeless projects and other local community ventures. Prior experiences of imprisonment varied from single substantial periods of incarceration to multiple brief sentences or a combination of both, served in a variety of penal institutions including Young Offender Institutions to High Security prisons. Consultants were all adults, with an age range from early 40s to late 50s.

Although we had given consideration to our expectations of the role consultants might fulfill within a formal 'role description', we had purposely kept this general, as there were no precedents to guide us, and the actual study itself was a feasibility study designed to explore the plethora of 'unknowns' around conducting research of this kind in the prison setting. We did not want to be too prescriptive, as it is known the levels of user involvement may change as a study progresses (Dixon, Peart, & Carr-Hill, 1999). We were determined to help support the creation of a milieu conducive to consultants feeling comfortable to share with us their perspectives of how the reality of life as a suicidal prisoner would need to be considered for the successful implementation of the study. We understood that to make this possible, a culture of collaboration based on mutual trust would be essential. Boote, Telford, and Cooper (2006), in discussing the impact of different hierarchies of user involvement, describe a continuum of levels of user involvement from low-level consultation processes where the power dynamic is weighted towards researcher control to higher levels of involvement based on an equal partnership with a shared power dynamic achievement through collaborative relationships. However, it is recognised that relationships take time to develop and, as Hanley et al. (2000) point out, users gain trust only as the study progresses.

Service user reference group meetings

Meetings were held monthly on University premises throughout the three-year period of the study. As with most new groups, our priority during early meetings was to get to know each other and negotiate a workable framework within which to operate. No doubt we all came to this novel project with some assumptions about criminality, research and Universities along with concerns of how, and even if, this melting pot of diversity would be successful. Early days were concerned with building relationships, and it soon became apparent that irrespective of our varied backgrounds, life opportunities and experiences our shared passion to improve services to help suicidal prisoners was paramount and became the defining feature underpinning all interactions.

As the facilitator of this group, I had no prior experience of working with ex-offenders but had made a commitment to myself that right from the start I would make every effort to shake off and reject any assumptions I may have acquired based on secondary sources such as media reports and would aim to approach this project with a spirit of naïve curiosity. Having a background as a clinician within the NHS, I was already comfortable with adopting a non-judgemental approach to patients in my care; however, another important premise here was that SURG members were not patients, nor were they research participants, so it was important to understand that here we aspired to develop a working relationship with each other as equal colleagues. Dewar (2005) describes a useful way of considering the relationship and specific skills and knowledge base of service users involved in research as 'equal but different' to researchers, suggesting that this demonstrates genuine respect and value for the contribution made by service users as opposed to tokenism. In the early days, meetings were chaired by the facilitator or another member of staff; however, in the last year of the study, members took it in turn to chair meetings following training from the study administrator.

Training and support needs

A principle that we had already adopted for other PPI groups within the School of Psychological Sciences at the University of Manchester was to ensure that, where needed, sufficient training was offered to lay members in order to equip them with the skills and knowledge required to make an effective contribution. The provision of 'training' for service user consultants is often overlooked in SURGs and, indeed, there exists a view among some researchers that service users somehow lose their 'service *user-ness*' and become 'professionalised' if they receive training about research. Cornes, Peardon, and Manthorpe (2008) along with Hanley et al. (2003) have alluded to a concern that service users who are involved in research may lose their objectivity, as the boundaries between researchers and users become blurred. However, this has been rejected by Wright, Corner, Hopkinson, and Foster (2006), who concede that a degree of so-called professionalisation is inevitable following training, but assert that this does not invalidate their service user status perspectives.

The issue of 'professionalisation' is not new and may be viewed akin to the phenomenon of 'going native', which was identified by early anthropological ethnographers who were sometimes accused of over-identifying with the jungle natives they were researching (Hobbs & May, 1993). More recently, the assumption that someone from a particular social group will automatically lose that perspective and normalize to the values and priorities of a new group has been questioned by Fuller (1999), who argues for the viability of a situation of 'multiple positionality' where the 'mixing and manipulating' of potentially competing identities can actually benefit all concerned by widening perspectives. The possibility that researchers who warn of the perils of 'professionalisation' may be uncomfortable with and feel threatened by the potential for a more equitable and less professionally dominated power balance in relationships must be considered.

Equally there are researchers who argue strongly in favour of the provision of training for service users involved in research. Telford, Beverley, Cooper, and Boote (2002) identify the provision of training for service users about research methodology as a key principle for successful patient and public involvement in research. Others, including Shah and Robinson

(2007) and Oliver et al. (2001), further argue that training of service users in research methods should be offered routinely.

The position we took was that our SURG members would be at an avoidable disadvantage if they had little understanding of the context we were now asking them to be involved in, and that there would be greater productivity from their contribution if they were more orientated towards research and allied issues. More generally, we also wished to support the personal professional development of members to foster the acquisition of additional knowledge and skills that would hold currency for future paid employment. To this effect, we introduced members to the 'Involvement Portfolio' developed by the NHS Research and Development Forum (2012) to help lay people involved in research recognise and record the new skills and knowledge being gained through such involvement activities.

One of the first challenges was to identify any training needs so that provision could be made to support the highest levels of SURG members' engagement and ability to make an effective contribution to the success of the research. To this effect, we carried out a Training Needs Analysis for each member soon after he or she had joined the group, using the template proforma produced by the Mental Health Research Network, existent at the time of the study. This is one of a number of excellent resources available within a Toolkit designed to support researchers who are involving service users in research (National Institute for Health Research, 2013). We found that SURG members already possessed a range of highly relevant skills prior to joining the group. Existing formal qualifications ranged from a Bachelor degree awarded from a Russell Group University, practitioner and trainer qualifications in a psychological therapy, and between them members had extensive voluntary experience of supporting the recovery of people with substance addictions and helping with homeless charities.

A number of potential training needs were identified, including:

- Information about the University
- Information about research
- Information about the topic of suicide prevention
- Information about clinical psychology and psychological therapies
- Information about formal meetings
- Information about presentation skills
- Information about IT, word processing, and so on.

As meetings were held in the University, and recognising that large formal institutions can be intimidating to many people, we provided information and training about the work of the University and how we would manage our meetings using an agenda and minutes. We further explained about 'meetings etiquette', outlining our expectations that members should send apologies if unable to attend and should come to meetings on time and well prepared by having read the minutes of last meeting in advance. It is important to note that we routinely discuss these issues with all new SURGs assisting the department to support both educational courses and other research studies and that this did not represent a special approach applied because service users came from a forensic background. All members were offered an Honorary Staff contract with the University in recognition of their role and to facilitate their access to training resources and support facilities to further their own personal development ambitions. The Honorary Staff contract was something that SURG members really valued, not solely on the basis of its currency in enabling access to training and other facilities but much more so as it appeared to represent a mark of societal respectability of being accepted by an esteemed formal institution.

Our colleagues from the School of Nursing, Midwifery and Social Work had already developed an excellent six-day research course suitable for lay advisors, which SURG members were allowed access to a place. This course consisted of the same lectures and workshops found within the Masters-level Research Methods course, but with the addition of a little extra mentoring and adapted course materials. All members elected to do the course and were paid for their time and travel from the study training budget. This really helped them understand the more technical aspects of the study and consequently their contributions were more informed. Other research training was delivered 'in house', including how to read a research paper (critical appraisal) and qualitative data analysis. Interestingly in the session on qualitative data analysis, a group exercise we carried out involved some experiential learning by coding a piece of data, and we found no difference in the codes ascribed by SURG members and research staff. Where particular training sessions were available at the University as Staff Training courses, we encouraged members to access these (e.g. Presentation skills course).

The core research staff team attended most SURG meetings, which were held at the University with the usual format of enjoying a buffet lunch together and then commencing the meeting by following the agenda items. The regular direct involvement of the Principle Investigator of the study seemed to be very important, as the type of information provided by SURG members was often of a nuanced nature, some of which would have been difficult to capture and convey within formal meeting minutes. As with any group, the trust required for strong effective relationships development takes time to achieve, and my sense was that as members had experienced situations in prison where they were dismissed or 'fobbed off' by prison staff perceived as low ranking, they appreciated having direct access to the study lead. Another issue within prison hierarchies is that the person in overall charge – the governor – was described by SURG members as having autocratic authority with lesser ranks having little autonomy. So in effect a feature of imprisonment may be that you learn that it's best to deal with the 'top man'!

Although meetings were informal and friendly, they were also business like, following a predetermined structure where we would provide an update on recent developments and then raise issues for which guidance or service user views and perspectives were sought in order to inform implementation of the study. All frontline researchers and academic co-investigators understood that they could attend meetings to draw on members' expertise at any time. This facility was well used, with requests for consultation ranging from guidance on how the research assistant should approach potential study participants to more formal involvement in the analysis of qualitative data.

Involvement activities

In the early stages of the study, preparation for recruitment of at-risk prisoners became the main priority, hence much attention and effort was applied to planning how to do this. The value of user guidance to assist in designing effective recruitment strategies is well documented (Angell et al. 2003; Barnard et al. 2005; Elliott, Watson, & Harries, 2002; Griffiths, Jorm, & Christensen, 2004; Hanley, Truesdale, King, Elbourne, & Chalmbers, 2001; Meyer, Torres, Cermeno, MacLean, & Monzon, 2003; Minkler et al., 2002), and particularly so with respect to hard-to-reach populations (Rhodes et al., 2002). Research assistants and trial therapists benefitted from advice about how to approach potential participants, for example ensuring privacy of the conversation to prevent a cell mate of other prisoners or staff from overhearing. Advice was also received concerning when to make approaches, including particular times to avoid such as association time, meal times, visiting times or when the prisoner was expecting a visit from his or her legal team.

We were constantly reminded of the scale of the problem of prisoners' poor literacy skills, with SURG members informing us of that such was the stigma of illiteracy that prisoners would be reluctant to be open about it for fear of ridicule or abuse and that we should be alert for covert illiteracy. This had implications for the way that researchers used research documents such as participant information sheets, consent forms and therapy materials, and it became clear that an assumption of adequate literacy could potentially result in poor recruitment, and that discussions around literacy would need to be handled with the utmost sensitivity.

Typically research staff would attend the monthly SURG meeting to present a draft plan for members to review and advise on. Cultural sensitivity to the situation of the participant has been shown to be important by Burrus, Liburd, and Burroughs (1998) and Smith et al. (2008), and guidance from SURG members on culturally sensitive practice was an invaluable component of their contribution throughout the entire research process. For example a recruitment flyer was produced to advertise the opportunity to participate in the study to prisoners. The first draft of this flyer featured written information about the study superimposed on a background picture of the prison building. On first sight of the flyer SURG members immediately told us of how they perceived the flyer as ugly and uninviting, explaining that prisoners were very aware of their incarceration within the ominous architecture of this building and that it would be unlikely to encourage anyone to take the time to read it. We were advised to choose something less emotively laden, which we did with their approval. This was one of a number of lessons that we were to learn related to how to make the best use of the expertise that SURG members had to offer. Initially our approach was to bring a draft of something to the group for their approval only to find that they identified difficulties that we had not predicted resulting in the need to make changes. Faulkner (2006) and others (Paterson 2004; Smith et al., 2008; Wright et al., 2006) have highlighted the need for attention to the detail with the language and wording of research documentation. This became relevant to us in a number of ways; for example in relation to a PhD study running alongside the main study where prisoners were required to complete a daily diary detailing aspects of their mood, feelings and other highly personal information into a formatted booklet. The researcher had prepared bespoke booklets with the logos of the University and the host NHS mental health trust on the cover and a range of instructions and scales for the prisoner to record the variables under study. Wording commonly used in participant information sheets and outcome measures for studies concerned with mental health were found to be inappropriate in this context. Even the term 'therapy' was considered potentially unacceptable for the prisoner population and, following SURG advice, was replaced by the term 'programme'. Once again, a number of really important issues were raised by SURG members who, viewing this through the lens of a suicidal prisoner, identified several issues requiring attention. First, we learned more about how suicidal inmates may be perceived by other prisoners as weak, open to exploitation and mockery and how the stigma of anything even remotely associated with mental health conditions was likely to invoke revulsion and victimization rather than understanding and compassion. This information brought with it a serious concern that without adequate understanding of the prison culture we could put already vulnerable prisoners at increased risk of psychological and physical abuse. The entire diary booklet needed revision; we were advised to amend the cover logos to remove any reference to 'mental', and we also received helpful advice about the presentation of the scales and use of more comprehensible language and lay terminology.

Alongside this, discussions opened up around the culture of rampant gossip where everyone knew everything about what should have been prisoners' personal affairs. More familiar concepts of privacy and confidentiality appeared non-existent in the prison, where acquisition of 'privileged' information served as currency to barter and gain cigarettes and other desired objects. The gossip culture thrives alongside suspicion, distrust and an underworld class system or hierarchy of prisoner status that must be respected to survive without harm. To translate this as it applies to the diary study, it was important that every possible measure was taken to uphold the safety of participants; therefore, planning of research assistant monitoring interviews involved ensuring complete privacy, as far as possible.

More generally to avoid fuelling the gossip culture, we were advised about not being seen to be too involved or friendly with the prison staff, of whom there was a great distrust amongst prisoners. Paradoxically we also needed to foster good relationships with prison officers to support the smooth running of the research; a necessity that SURG members fully understood. However, throughout many SURG meetings, members repeatedly stressed the need to be seen by prisoners as being completely independent of prison structures. They also gave other valuable guidance about ways of promoting acceptance amongst prisoners, including dressing casually, and gave advice of definitely not wearing formal business suits, which prisoners would associate with the senior prison management. Advice was also provided to keep research staff safe in the prison, with warnings of the types of prisoner to be very cautious about being alone in a room or cell with. Working in a system where distrust is the norm created challenges when attempting to engage prisoners in the research and the therapy. SURG members strongly advised of the need to never let a participant down on something that had been previously agreed. This was very difficult at times when an interview or therapy session had to be cancelled due to prison matters completely outside the control of the research team. This resulted in being advised to prepare participants for such an eventuality by discussing this right at the start.

Much information was suggested to promote good participant care, especially so for dealing with a situation that manifested when we found that some participants who were receiving therapy were transferred out to another prison despite the authorities having already agreed to a 'medical holding order' ensuring that the prisoner participants' course of therapy would not be interrupted or prematurely discontinued. Members were very concerned at how a prisoner who was in therapy would react to the stress of not only a sudden transfer to a different prison but also the unplanned cessation of therapy. This was felt to present the potential for increasing the participant's risk of suicide, as sensitive personal issues may have been raised in therapy leaving no opportunity for these to be safely managed. There were also fears that risk could be raised by increasing the participant's sense of rejection and abandonment. It was decided to make strenuous representations to the prison management to reinforce the importance of reneging on agreed protocols but also to write to the transferred prisoner and new prison to explain what had happened.

Members were also keen to help with developing the therapy for this population and offered the trial therapists valuable advice and guidance when problems arose. For example it had been noticed that some participants in the intervention group were difficult to engage in therapy and some had dropped out. The therapy is derived from a manual first developed for a community-based sample that had a history of suicidality but were not currently suicidal; therefore, it was expected that it would need some adaptation appropriate for the different population being treated in the prison. Members advised that the attention span of most prisoners in that situation may be severely compromised due to a combination of factors and that it would be worth trying to break the course of therapy into smaller components. This resulted in dividing the course into five discreet 'therapy modules' and offering the participant a choice of which module he or she would like to prioritize to work on. This proved successful, with subsequent participants engaging better and less attrition.

Another very successful contribution from members was to help with dissemination of the research and its outputs. All members were involved in developing the content of presentations and delivering the presentation itself at Research and Development seminars. On both occasions, the seminars were over-booked with attendees and were very well evaluated by attending clinical, academic and other professional staff. On another occasion, a SURG member accompanied the research team to a different prison where we aspired to carry out research in the future, and the member achieved great engagement and rapport with the audience.

Attendance at monthly SURG meetings was exceptionally high, with most members rarely missing a meeting. This was despite two members continuing to spend brief periods in prison. Sadly, during the last year of the study we lost contact with one member who appeared to drop out from the group.

Challenges

Sometimes SURG members became frustrated with the slow speed of progress with the organizational issues mainly related to prison security regulations that served as obstacles to the study. Frequently, as part of the routine update on general progress of the study, they would hear the same problems with little progress, and sometimes this would manifest as anger at the perceived injustice and a disregard of prison bureaucracy for the psychological well-being of the prisoner participants.

Sometimes we felt rather frustrated that tasks that we allocated to members to be worked on between meetings were rarely accomplished (e.g. members were asked to produce a brief outline of their personal profile for a presentation that they were to deliver). However, we came to view this frustration as a learning point that it was best to schedule all necessary work into meetings times.

On just a few occasions, one member brought personal issues into meeting discussions but responded to a gentle reminder of the ground rules; however, this can happen sometimes even within our other non-forensic PPI groups. A strategy that we developed to avoid excessive deviance away for agenda items was to have the first item as 'Members Check-in', as this allowed for members to give an update of what they had been doing in between meetings and then agree to concentrate on research-related issues.

A major challenge both for individual members and for the research team was to find a way of paying SURG members for their time, as NHS Trust and University financial standing orders were not originally designed to accommodate PPI, and such payments were usually made by direct transfer into a bank account or via a personal cheque. As some members had legal restrictions prohibiting them having a bank account, this proved problematic. Eventually a less than desirable but workable solution of gifting cash payments to members at each meeting was implemented.

Impact

An increasingly important body of knowledge is now accessible to guide researchers towards designing studies that can be translated into mainstream clinical practice and thereby demonstrate a positive meaningful effect of their end beneficiaries lives. Implementation science exists to develop and apply theoretical models to improve the uptake of research findings into practice (Bero et al., 1998). This is particularly important in the current climate of public and political scrutiny of the cost and value for money of publically funded institutions such as universities and the National Health Service. In 2006, Sir David Cooksey published a report commissioned by the Treasury to investigate the impact of research funding; the report highlighted excessive levels of waste arising from the lack of uptake of publically funded research (Cooksey, 2006). Cooksey citied two major 'translation gaps' responsible for preventing the application of appropriate research findings. The first gap concerns lack of progression of empirical laboratory-based research into a clinical application, and the second translation gap refers to lack of application of evidence-based knowledge into clinical practice. Aligned to implementation science is knowledge mobilization (or the theory of how individuals make decisions and judgements about how or whether to *mobilize* knowledge into action in terms of clinical practice behaviours). Both paradigms are concerned with effective change management underpinned by a strong message of the importance of stakeholder involvement and collaborative partnership working throughout all stages of the inception, design and delivery of new developments. As end beneficiaries of health research, service users are the largest yet least represented population of stakeholders, others being commissioners, clinicians, academics and so on. One of the main drivers for PPI in clinical research concerns the need to develop interventions that are 'fit for purpose' in that they meet the needs of 'real people' with 'real-life' problems living in 'real-life situations'. The oft lack of translation of the gold standard randomised controlled trial into everyday practice has been identified by the Medical Research Council (MRC) as a challenge for researchers. The MRC guidelines for developing and evaluating complex intervention (MRC, 2008) stress the need for greater attention to feasibility and acceptability issues in order to produce interventions that work as well in the real world as within the sterile scientific bubble of the experiment. The value of consumer or PPI in research revolves around using the opportunity to test out researcher generated ideas against the reality of real people's views and experiences. However, to do this well and generate contributions with utility requires considerable effort and resources in terms of skilled and knowledgeable staff and service user consultants. Indeed, PPI itself has been described as a complex intervention by Brett et al. (2010), as it involves multiple levels of interfacing variables. PPI in research done well requires skilled facilitation by staff possessing a sense of compassion, tolerance, curiosity, appreciation of humour, patience, enthusiasm, resilience and humility. In addition, the knowledge and skills of interpersonal communication, relationship development, group dynamics and andragogy are core.

Recently, attention of the research community has moved from criticizing or advocating for PPI to considering the impact of PPI in research. This field of enquiry tends to straddle the two domains of impact of service user involvement on the research process to impact of being involved in research on the service user. Literature to demonstrate an objective 'scientific' quantifiable outcome measure is lacking at present (Telford & Faulkner, 2004); a situation which fuels perpetuation of the debate of whether PPI is good science or merely carried out for political correctness. Good ethics is synonymous with good science, and users can offer 'lived experience' expertise helpful in ensuring avoidance of participant excess burden or distress.

In retrospect, it would have been better if we had been able to consult with forensic service users during the development of the research proposal, because time and resources could have been used more economically by getting research processes right the first time rather than having to redesign protocols when they proved to be ineffective.

Other opportunities

SURG members were offered several opportunities to be involved in other forensic research studies from a range of our academic colleagues as a result of the campus grapevine! We were very pleased that their expertise was seen to be of potential benefit to other studies; however, we did have some unfounded concerns of whether the exceptional commitment and enthusiasm they had shown to the PROSPeR study would be affected.

Conclusion

Overall, we look back on three years of discovery and learning that was always stimulating in that meetings possessed a special vibrancy not as apparent in other PPI group meetings, fascinating in that we gained knowledge of the everyday lives of a population that many of us would not normally expect to meet, but also filled with extremes of utter sadness at the tragedies of circumstances that had led to some members becoming prisoners balanced with great humour at times when SURG members sometimes recounted comical anecdotes of their past encounters. We have been privileged to work with some exceptional individuals who have successfully turned around past criminal lifestyles to become productive members of mainstream society – in as much as society will allow them. Throughout the three years, for all of us, some myths have been blown away and some assumptions and prejudices have been challenged as we negotiated our way to develop effective working relationships. We have ended the project not with sadness but with a sense of optimism and renewed determination to plan for a larger scale definitive trial.

References

Angell, K., Kreshka M., McCoy R., Donnelly P., Turner-Cobb J., Graddy K., . . . Koopman, C. (2003). Psychosocial intervention for rural women with breast cancer: The Sierra-Stanford Partnership. *Journal of General Internal Medicine, 18*(7), 499–507.

Barnard, A., Carter, M., Britten, N., Purtell, R., Wyatt, K., & Ellis, A. (2005). *The PC11 Report. An evaluation of consumer involvement in the London Primary Care Studies Programme.* Exeter, UK. Peninsula Medical School.

Bero, L., Grilli, R., Grimshaw, J., Harvey, G., Oxman, A., & Thomson, M. (1998). Closing the gap between research and practice: An overview of systematic reviews of interventions to promote implementation of research findings. *British Medical Journal, 317*, 465–468.

Boote, J., Telford, R., & Copper, C. (2006). Principles and indicators of successful consumer involvement in NHS research: Results of a Delphi study and sub-group analysis. *Health Policy, 755*(3), 280–297.

Brett, J., Stanszewska, S., Mockford, C., Seers, K., Herron-Marx, S., & Bayliss, H. (2010). *The PIRICOM study: A systematic review of the measurement, impact and outcomes of patients and public involvement in health and social care research.* London, UK: Clinical Research Collaboration.

Burrus, B.B., Liburd, L., & Burroughs, A. (1998). Maximizing participation by black Americans in population-based diabetes research: The Project DIRECT pilot experience. *Journal of Community Health, 23*(1), 15–27.

Cooksey, D. (2006). *A review of UK health research funding.* London, UK: HMSO.

Cornes, M., Peardon, J., & Manthorpe, J. (2008). Wise owls and professors: The role of older researchers in the review of the National Service Framework for older people. *Health Expectations, 11*(4), 409–417.

Dewar, B. (2005). Beyond tokenistic involvement of older people in research – a framework for future development and understanding. *Journal of Clinical Nursing, 14*(3a), 48–53.

Dixon, P., Peart, E., & Carr-Hill, R. (1999). *A database of examples of consumer involvement in research.* York, UK: University of York.

Elliott, E., Watson, A., & Harries, U. (2002). Harnessing expertise: Involving peer interviewers in qualitative research with hard-to-reach populations. *Health Expectations, 10*, 339–348.

Faulkner, A. (2006). *Beyond our expectations: A report of the experiences of involving service users in forensic mental health research. National Programme on Forensic Mental Health Research and Development.* London, UK: Department of Health.

Fuller, D. (1999). Part of the action, or 'going native'? Learning to cope with the 'politics of integration'. *Area, 31*(3), 221–227.

Griffiths, K., Jorm, A., & Christensen, H. (2004). Academic consumer researchers: A bridge between consumers and researchers. *Australian and New Zealand Journal of Psychiatry, 38*(4), 191–196.

Hanley, B., Bradburn J., Barnes, M., Evans, C., Goodare, H., Kelson, M., . . . Wallcraft, J. (2003). *Involving the public in NHS, Public Health and Social Care Research: Briefing notes for researchers* (2nd ed.). Eastleigh, UK. INVOLVE.

Hanley, B., Bradburn, J., Gorin, S., Barnes, M., Evans, C., Goodare, H., . . . Wallcraft, J. (2000). *Involving consumers in research and development in the NHS: Briefing notes for Researchers.* Winchester, UK: The Help for Health Trust.

Hanley, B., Truesdale, A., King, A., Elbourne, D., & Chalmers, I. (2001). Involving consumers in designing, conducting and interpreting randomised controlled trials: Questionnaire survey. *British Medical Journal, 322*(7285), 519–523.

Hobbs, R., & May, T. (Eds). (1993). *Interpreting the field; accounts of ethnography.* Oxford, UK: Oxford University Press.

INVOLVE. (2014). *About INVOLVE introduction.* Retrieved from www.invo.org.uk.

Medical Research Council [MRC]. (2008). *Developing and evaluating complex interventions: New guidance.* London, UK: Author.

Meyer, M., Torres, S., Cermeno, N., MacLean, L., & Monzon, R. (2003). Immigrant women implementing participatory research in health promotion. *Western Journal of Nursing Research, 25*(7), 815–834.

Minkler, M., Fadem, P., Perry, M., Blum, K., Moore, L., & Rogers, J. (2002). Ethical dilemmas in participatory action research: A case study from the disability community. *Health Education and Behavior, 29*(1), 14–29.

National Institute for Health Research. (2013). *Good practice guidance for involving people with experience of mental health problems in research.* Retrieved from www.rds-sw.nihr.ac.uk/documents/NIHR_MHRN_Involving_Mental_Health_Problems_Research2013.pdf

National Survivor User Network. (2011). *Unlocking service user involvement practices in forensic settings. Research into the provision of service user involvement in secure settings.* London, UK: NSUN and WISH.

NHS Research and Development Forum. (2012). *Involvement portfolio.* Retrieved from www.rdforum.nhs.uk

Oliver, S., Milne, R., Bradburn, J., Buchanan, P., Kerridge, L., Walley, T., & Gabbay, J. (2001). Involving consumers in a needs-led research programme: a pilot project. *Health Expectations, 4*(1), 18–28.

Paterson, C. (2004). 'Take small steps to go a long way' consumer involvement in research into complementary and alternative therapies. *Complementary Therapies in Nursing, 1394,* 403–413.

Rhodes, P., Nocon, A., Booth, M., Chowdrey, M.Y., Fabian, A., Lambert, N., . . . Walgrove, T. (2002). A service users' research advisory group from the perspectives of both service users and researchers. *Health and Social Care in Community, 10*(5), 402–409.

Shah, S., & Robinson, I. (2007). Benefits of and barriers to involving users in medical device technology development and evaluation. *International Journal of Technology Assessment in Health Care, 23*(1), 131–137.

Smith, E., Ross, F., Donovan, S., Manthorpe, J., Brearley, S., Sitzia, J., & Beresford, P. (2008). Service user involvement in nursing, midwifery and health visiting research: a review of evidence and practice. *International Journal of Nursing Studies, 45*(2), 298–315.

Spiers, S., Harvey, K., & Chivers, C. (2005). Service user involvement in forensic mental health: Can it work? *Journal of Forensic Psychiatry and Psychology, 16*(2), 211–220.

Telford, R., Beverley, C., Copper, C., & Boote, J. (2002). What does it mean to involve consumers successfully in NHS research? A consensus study. *Health Expectations, 7*(3), 209–220.

Telford, R., & Faulkner, A. (2004). Learning about service use involvement in mental health research. *Mental Health, 13*(6), 549–559.

Wright, D., Corner, J., Hopkinson, J., & Foster, C. (2006). Listening to the views of people affected by cancer about cancer research: An example of participatory research in setting the cancer research agenda. *Health Expectations, 9*(1), 3–12.

7 Overcoming the challenges of implementing psychological interventions for the prevention of suicide in a prison setting

Daniel Pratt

Background

Prisoners are identified as a high-risk group in the National Suicide Prevention Strategy for England (Department of Health, 2002), and the development of evidence-based suicide prevention interventions for prisoners is highly recommended. However, there are no evidence-based psychological interventions routinely available for this group. Despite the dearth of interventions, clinical psychologists and psychological therapists working in prisons and other forensic settings are well placed to play an important role in the prevention of future suicides. The current situation presents clinical psychology with an opportunity to rise to a long-standing challenge and offer a different perspective on the assessment and intervention of vulnerable prisoners at risk of suicide. The aim for such preventative interventions would be to provide short-term benefits to vulnerable individuals coping with suicidal ideation within a prison environment, and longer term gains through the development of resilience to future suicidal behaviour that would protect the individual following his or her release from prison into the general community. Such psychological interventions would also be expected to benefit those prison staff who provide care and support for at-risk prisoners.

As described in Chapter 4, we have recently investigated the feasibility and acceptability of implementing a new psychological intervention for suicidal prisoners (Pratt et al., in press). Whilst doing this work, we became aware of a range of challenges facing the therapist that have to be addressed for the interventions to be most effectively delivered. We understood these obstacles as relating to the demands of the institution and the context of working within the prison environment, as well as the more specific vulnerabilities and distresses presented by the individuals with which the therapist was working. We argue these contextual and individual issues need to be recognised and responded to for psychological interventions to be well received by the prisoners and to be supported by the prison staff.

This chapter will hold a practical focus upon the most pertinent challenges affecting the implementation of psychological interventions for the prevention of suicide in prison settings. Throughout, we hope to offer some helpful considerations and suggestions to the therapist faced with overcoming such challenges.

Contextual challenges

Consideration of the contextual impact of being in prison on the vulnerable individual accessing psychological therapy is of upmost importance (Haney, 2005; Harvey & Smedley, 2010). The delivery of psychological interventions from a purely individualistic perspective would be insufficient and disallow meaningful engagement with the prisoner. Pertinent systemic factors, such as the quality of the regime, staff-prisoner relationships, safety, care and family contact (Harvey, 2011), should be included within the case formulation to allow the collaborative psychological work to realistically identify targets for change. Acting as an advocate by requesting the reduction/removal of contextual stressors considered to be maintaining the prisoner's suicidal ideation and behaviour may be the single most important role of the psychologist.

Of course, psychologists are not detached from this context; indeed, they are likely to be seen by the prisoner as 'part of the system'. As such, they would benefit from developing their own self-awareness of where they fit within this system. As is commonly the case in the UK, many clinical psychologists and psychological therapists are employed by an external service, often the NHS, but placed 'into the prison' for the purposes of treatment delivery. It is imperative for therapists employed in such a manner to ingratiate themselves with the ways of working of the prison, by regularly attending care team meetings, prison management meetings and case reviews and opportunistically shadowing prison staff. This demonstrable commitment serves two aims: first, psychologists become aware of the culture and 'moral performance' (Liebling, 2004) of the prison in which they are based, and second, therapists are developing a role and position within the establishment from which they may need to draw influence over the immediate environment experienced by prisoners whom the psychologists are working with therapeutically. Without demonstration of a commitment to the broader work of the prison, which hopefully leads to an acceptance of the psychologist's position within the prison's systems, contextual change is unlikely to follow from any requests.

In order to begin engaging prisoners in a new therapeutic programme (e.g. CBT for suicidal prisoners), psychological therapists should spend time on the prison wings to familiarise themselves with the 'wing culture' and also to become known to prisoners and staff on the wing. Developing a human relationship with staff and prisoners on the wing is often a necessary pre-requisite for a therapeutic relationship to become possible. Referrals tend to be made between the staff/prisoner and the individual therapists, rather than to a faceless therapeutic programme.

Each individual prison wing tends to be manned by different sets of staff and houses different categories of prisoners, such as drug-free, vulnerable prisoners, reception wing and so on. As such, wings tend to develop their own cultures, ways of working and codes of attitudes and acceptable behaviours. On some wings, there can be considerable pressure for new staff and prisoners joining the wing to conform to this existing culture and, because acceptance into the wing community is of paramount importance to most new staff and prisoners, acculturation activities are often agreed to by the newcomer. This is an important contextual issue for the therapist, perhaps considered to be an outsider to this culture, because he or she is dependent on new referrals of prisoners seeking treatment and also because some aspects of the psychological intervention may work better if the staff on the wing can work alongside the prisoner in developing alternative ways of thinking or coping.

Remaining aware of the context within which the therapist is working is important when the delivery of therapy to prisoners is interrupted, disrupted and even discontinued because of matters outside the control of both the therapist and the client. For instance lockdowns caused by a perceived security risk can be a common occurrence in some prisons and restrict prisoner and staff movements within the prison as well as into and out of the establishment. Also, because of the variable nature of the prison setting, the risk status of the prisoner client may also be changeable and he or she may be considered by prison staff to be unsuitable or 'too risky' for a therapy session on the day of the appointment. These considerations need to be made in addition to the usual reasons for Did Not Attends (DNAs) when delivering therapy in the community.

A model of delivering therapy in 50–60 minute sessions may present a challenge to some parts of the prison setting. Typically in a healthcare centre, the medical model and approach to patient appointments has a long-standing history and prevalent usage. Therefore, prison staff may understandably hold an expectation that psychologists working in healthcare will fit into this existing way of working, that is 10-minute appointments, frequent interruptions, larger number of patients seen in each clinic session. The preference for a therapist to hold a clinic for only three clients who they expect to see for up to an hour at a time without interruption may need to be sensitively communicated to prison staff. In our experience, this different way of working is respected by prison staff once they are made aware, although developing this awareness may be a challenge if prisoner movements to the healthcare centre are facilitated by temporary staff on an overtime rota.

An alternative to using the healthcare centre for the delivery of therapy, which may also mirror the increasing preference in the community to hold outpatient therapy sessions away from hospital sites (Holmes, 2010; Maxfield & Segal, 2008), is to arrange access to workshop facilities or locations used by offender occupational/rehabilitation programmes. Although the majority of the workshop spaces available for use provide vocational training programmes such as bricklaying, plastering and so on, we have previously been fortunate to secure use of a workshop space that was equipped with small office rooms designed to be used for appointments with external agencies such as social workers, probation staff and solicitor visits. Whilst not ideal, we have found such spaces to be suitable for psychological therapy and less stigmatizing for the prisoner than attending the healthcare centre for 'mental health treatment', which can often be seen by other prisoners as a sign of weakness to be exploited.

As is the case for any psychological therapy, not all clients will pursue a full course of the intervention and may prefer to terminate their therapy early for a variety of reasons. The withdrawal from therapy by a prisoner has to be carefully and sensitively communicated to the prison staff on the prisoner's wing and to the prison system as a whole. In the community, the early termination of therapy caused by the client's withdrawal can be construed in various ways, such as the client being insufficiently psychologically prepared for the therapy at the present time, too much instability in the client's life to allow for reflective working, concurrent demands on the client's time negating the possibility of attending appointments and so on. Because one of the primary roles of the prison is to demonstrate it is carrying out its responsibility of contributing to the rehabilitation of their prisoners, a prisoner terminating treatment early may be construed in a different way. Non-attendance or withdrawal from therapy may be considered to be 'refusal to engage' and then seen as an indicator that the prisoner is resistant to rehabilitation, which may have a detrimental impact on any parole board hearing. Therefore, even if the therapist is taking a collaborative approach to his or her work with the prisoner client, the dynamics of the wider system need to be considered when providing therapy within a prison setting (Harvey & Smedley, 2010).

A frequent frustration experience by therapists working within a prison setting is the unexpected or unplanned release of prisoners during treatment. This issue presents a considerable challenge to the successful completion of a treatment contact and the collection of post-treatment assessment data useful for evaluation purposes. Although the degree of this challenge differs across the various remits and types of prisons, prisoners are often released or transferred before the expected discharge date with little, if any, notice provided to the psychologist (Lane, Goldstein, Heilbrun, Cruise, & Pennacchia, 2012). The impact of this issue can be reduced, to some extent, by tailoring the delivery of the interventions (e.g. frequency of therapy sessions) to allow for the prisoner's individual circumstances in order to the increase the likelihood of a full intervention being completed (Mulcahy, Krezmien, Leone, Houchins, & Baltodano, 2008). Additionally, ongoing communication with prison staff concerning discharge dates can help to reduce attrition and to prevent causing detrimental effect on the prisoner's care and support following release (Hammett, Roberts, & Kennedy, 2001).

An issue encountered early in our work in delivering the Cognitive Behavioural Suicide Prevention (CBSP) therapy to prisoners at risk of suicide is the potential for some prisoners to be judged by prison staff as *manipulative* or *attention-seeking*. The management of manipulative inmates is a frustrating and draining challenge regularly faced by prison staff, and it is not unusual for prisoners to call attention to themselves by stating they are suicidal, threatening to make an attempt, to be transferred to the healthcare centre or local hospital (Hayes, 1993). Amongst those investigating the prevention of suicidal behaviour, there is a prevailing sense that anyone making threats of suicide or even engaging in suicidal behaviour, including self-harm, could be identified as on the continuum of suicidal behaviour and experiencing distress that would warrant further assessment, at least. However, amongst prison staff, there has been a long-standing view that suicidal threats and self-harming behaviour is 'a manipulative tactic' designed to gain cell relocation or to avoid a reduction in privileges (Toch, 1975). This apparent difference in viewpoints has to be carefully managed by the therapist working with 'suicidal prisoners'. In our work, we were aware of the potential for some prisoners to use various strategies to gain advantage over others within the constraints of the prison system; however, we agree with Toch (1977) that *all* acts of suicidal behaviour should be seen as indicative of personal breakdowns resulting from crises of self-doubt, poor coping and problem-solving skills, hopelessness and fear of abandonment.

It is important for the treating therapist to remain aware of any key events that have recently occurred with the prisoner, such as cell relocations, prisoner violence either involving or observed by the prisoner or suicidal behaviour by the prisoner or others known to them. Such events are likely to have an impact on the prisoner's current mental health and well-being and his or her capacity to engage in more reflective or demanding aspects of therapy. By remaining aware of key events, the therapist can tailor and adapt the pace and course of each therapy session accordingly. Similarly, the therapist must remain aware of the context the prisoner will be re-entering immediately after the end of the therapy session. In CBSP sessions, therapists would ensure the final 5 or 10 minutes of each session were not distressing or challenging for the prisoner, perhaps moving the conversation onto more everyday topics, such as television programmes or sports. We also recognise the potential benefit to the prisoner of engaging in a 'grounding' exercise during this time, which allows the individual to re-familiarise himself or herself with the 'prisoner role' and the need to put the 'prison mask' back on.

As highlighted earlier, there are likely to be a number of differences between the ways of working, cultures and personal standpoints held by prison staff and the incoming psychologist working with prisoners to reduce distress. For this reason, we have found it to be important to develop effective working relationships with each level of the prison staff hierarchy, from the prison officer on the wing in everyday contact with suicidal prisoners through to the Prison Governors/Administrators with responsibility for ensuring the safety of all staff and prisoners. We have striven to work alongside our prison colleagues to emphasise our shared interests and goals in preventing suicidality and reducing prisoner distress. Effective relationships between prison staff and psychological therapists are essential given the likelihood of prisoner suicidal behaviour during the delivery of the intervention and the subsequent need to openly discuss sensitive material affecting the prisoner's ongoing care and support.

Individual challenges

When engaging prisoners in psychological therapy, the institutional demands on the individual (both explicit and implicit) need to be considered. Individuals with no previous history of imprisonment will be at the early stages of adaptation to prison life and are likely, therefore, to require the psychologist's approach to be more sensitive to his or her existing levels of distress and reduced capacity for detailed reflection. In comparison, a long-term prisoner who has developed a firmer sense of identity and understanding of the demands of the prison regime and culture may be more able to respond to a demanding course of psychological therapy, although additional consideration would then need to be made of how extended periods of time in prison have affected the prisoner's view of self, the world and his or her future.

Prisons can be extremely dangerous places from which there is no exit or escape. Prisoners, therefore, need to learn quickly and become aware of the potential dangers within their environment. They learn to become hyper-vigilant of any possible indicators of personal threat or danger. In order to maintain personal safety and integrity, this can result in an individual adaptively becoming distrustful of others and suspicious of others' intentions. A hyper-vigilant, distrusting individual may also benefit from projecting an image of himself or herself as 'tough' or 'hard' because this reduces the likelihood of being dominated or exploited by other prisoners (McCorkle, 1992). Furthermore, to protect oneself from victimisation from other prisoners, an individual may feel the need to suppress his or her emotional responses to internal and external environmental events. Some prisoners can become emotionally over-controlled and develop a 'prison mask' that is unrevealing and impenetrable in order to ensure he or she is not seen as weak and vulnerable (Haney, 2003). Whilst this interpersonal style may be adaptive and helpful to the prisoner in coping with imprisonment, it can present a challenge to both the therapist and prisoner client aiming to engage in a piece of reflective, exposing therapy. The development of trust with prisoners can be a slow process requiring considerable patience from the therapist, who should expect to be 'tested' by the prisoner along the way as he or she gradually feels more comfortable in making important disclosures about past and current experiences and related emotions. The regularity of contact and consistency of non-judgemental responses to such disclosures can be important in supporting the ongoing development of the trusting therapeutic relationship.

Most prisoners have no previous experience of psychological therapy. Indeed, many prisoners have little, if any, previous involvement with health services either in prison or in the community. The high levels of pre-existing unmet health needs have attracted prisoner groups the label of the 'hard-to-reach' sector of society (Department of Health and HM Prison Service, 2002). The approach made by psychologists to engaging prisoners in psychological therapy needs to be mindful of this lack of experience, with their approach tailored accordingly. Even the use of vocabulary commonly accepted within community settings may be inappropriate or off-putting to prisoners. We have found the use of the word 'therapy' to be a case in point here. As such, we moved to offering prisoners the opportunity to take part in a 'programme' to help people cope with suicidal thoughts and feelings whilst in prison. The word 'programme' was seen as more acceptable to prisoners because it was often used to describe a number of other activities available to them, including educational programmes (e.g. literacy and numeracy skills), vocational programmes (e.g. bricklaying, plastering) and offending behaviour programmes (e.g. enhanced thinking skills). By using existing vocabulary to describe the new therapy, a more positive response of prisoners enrolling on the 'programme' was received.

At times, it can be particularly challenging and frustrating when attempting to engage a prisoner in a psychological intervention. Although one may assume that there is more than enough opportunity for the prisoner to find time in his or her weekly schedule to attend therapy sessions and complete homework tasks, therapists must be extremely creative in their approach to engaging prisoners in this work as they strive to develop a trusting, open and honest therapeutic relationship. The therapist may wish to draw upon principles from Motivational Interviewing when working with prisoners who seem to be more difficult to engage (McMurran, 2002; Miller & Rollnick, 2002; Rollnick, Miller, & Butler, 2008). 'Rolling with resistance' and validating the prisoner's experience, whilst not colluding with the prisoner's judgements of such experience, can enable the therapist to develop the context for the prisoner to feel able to more openly express his or her views without fear of negative judgement of weakness or vulnerability that may be expected from fellow prisoners.

Specific consideration needs to be made of one of the common challenges experienced by psychologists working in prisons and other secure settings – that is clients' completion and discussion of written tasks between therapy sessions (Eccleston & Sorbello, 2002; Smedley, 2010). Such tasks, especially the completion of homework exercises within a cognitive behavior therapy (CBT) intervention, can offer significant advantages to the delivery of CBT and yet also pose a significant threat to the prisoner's continued engagement in the therapy. Whilst this can be an issue faced outside of correctional settings, it seems to be a major barrier to engagement when working with prisoners. Prisoner literacy rates are known to be poor (Davies, Lewis, Byatt, Purvis, & Cole, 2004), with a majority of prisoners unable to demonstrate a reading ability that would be expected of an 11-year-old leaving primary school. Therefore, skill deficits in reading and writing contribute to the incompletion of typical CBT worksheets such as thought records and activity schedules.

Furthermore, many prisoners did not have a positive schooling experience and a reminder of this, and confirmation of their limited academic skills, can undermine their motivation to complete homework. Prisoners' use of avoidance of 'failure experiences' may have developed as a coping strategy to protect their fragile self-esteem. Because homework tasks can provide the opportunity to improve client motivation and mood, to gather real-time information on key thoughts, feelings and beliefs, and to test out new ways of coping within a no-lose behavioural experiment, the therapist working with prisoners needs to be particularly creative in how such tasks are designed and delivered. It is often necessary to dispel any prisoner-held myths about the likely evaluative judgements the therapist will hold about their completed homework. Praise and positive reinforcement of any completed tasks should be heavily emphasised initially to ensure disconfirmation of this myth.

As is the case for therapists working with any client group, there is a legal and ethical responsibility for sharing risk-pertinent information as soon as this becomes known to them. Client confidentiality is sought to be maintained throughout a course of treatment, although confidentiality breaches are mandated when disclosures of risk information are made. When working within a prison setting, the need to breach confidentiality is extended beyond the usual 'risk to self' and 'risk to others' domains to also include 'risk to the security of the establishment'. Clearly maintaining the safety and security of the institution must be of paramount importance and, therefore, the need for such a breach may have to be carefully explained to the prisoner. Although consent procedures must outline reasons for confidentiality breaches prior to the commencement of treatment, the psychologist would be advised to pay additional attention to the therapeutic relationship during such disclosures. There would be a preference to include the prisoner in the disclosure of security information (in a phone call, meeting or the preparation of paperwork) to the relevant personnel within the prison, although some prisoners may feel upset or reluctant to be involved in the reporting procedure. Nevertheless, confidentiality breaches must always be prioritised even if this is at the expense of this relationship and likely to lead to the prisoner prematurely withdrawing from treatment. Additionally, psychologists and prison staff should work closely in order to agree to a reporting procedure to be followed for disclosures. Preferably, these would be consistent with existing reporting policies and procedures required by the institution thus preventing tension developing between psychologists and prison staff supporting the prison during this procedure (Lane et al., 2012).

Tailoring the delivery of CBT for suicide within a prison environment

- The psychologist must remain aware of the impact of imprisonment upon the client.

  ○ Systemic and contextual factors should be considered within the formulation.
  ○ Creative solutions may be required to overcome environmental restrictions.

- 'Walking the wings' can demonstrate the psychologist's commitment to working within the prison setting and facilitate acceptance within the staff and prisoner culture.
- Accommodation has to be secured that offers uninterrupted privacy.
- Assertive engagement of prisoners in CBT may be required and non-attendance at sessions and withdrawal from therapy should be managed with an awareness of the potential implications this may have upon the prisoner's sentence plan.
- Some suicidal prisoners may attract judgements from staff as being manipulative or attention seeking. Differences in perspectives on the management of suicidal prisoners have to be sensitively negotiated without the psychologist distancing himself or herself from the staff or prisoner.
- An individualised assessment of the impact of imprisonment on the client is warranted.
- The psychologist must be sensitive to the prisoner's current level of distress and imported vulnerabilities.
- The client's 'prison mask' can be adaptive when coping with imprisonment.
- Getting behind the mask is important for the emotional benefits of CBT to be experienced, although the therapist must ensure the client is sufficiently self-protected again before leaving the session.
- A trusting client-therapist alliance can take considerable time to develop. Regularity of predictable contact and consistency of non-judgemental responses to the prisoner's disclosures are important.
- A prisoner's lack of familiarity with psychological therapy may require the psychologist's approach to be tailored, with a slow pace of initial engagement often well received.
- The prisoner's literacy ability may influence willingness to engage in CBT, as such non-completion of homework tasks should be sensitively explored with the individual.

Conclusions

Prisoners are a high-risk group for suicide. Elevated rates of suicidal behaviour in prison can be explained by the high levels of complex mental health problems interacting with an environment that is experienced as frightening, desperate and hopeless, and one that encourages hyper-vigilance, social and emotional withdrawal and an outwardly over-masculine 'prison mask'.

Currently, there are no evidence-based psychological interventions targeting suicidal behaviour routinely available to prisoners, and yet improving the health and well-being of prisoners has a number of public health implications. Prisoners are often from marginalised populations that have poor access to healthcare in the community; therefore, periods of incarceration offer important opportunities to provide much-needed prevention and treatment interventions. a variety of prevention and treatment interventions. The delivery of evidence-based suicide prevention interventions for prisoners is recommended (Department of Health, 2002; US Department of Health and Human Services, 2001).

Despite numerous individual and contextual issues making psychotherapeutic work with prisoners difficult and challenging, there remains a desperate need to develop and evaluate new psychological interventions specifically targeting distress associated with suicidal ideation and behaviour experienced by prisoners. This research theme should fundamentally improve the way such vulnerable patients are treated and reduce the economic and social costs of inefficient or ineffective treatments for these patients in other services.

References

Davies, K., Lewis, J., Byatt, J., Purvis, E., & Cole, B. (2004). *An evaluation of the literacy demands of general offending behaviour programmes.* London, UK: Home Office Development and Statistics Directorate (Report No. 233).

Department of Health. (2002). *National suicide prevention strategy for England.* London, UK: Author.

Department of Health and HM Prison Service. (2002). *Developing and modernising primary care in prisons.* London, UK: Author.

Eccleston, L., & Sorbello, L. (2002). The RUSH program – real understanding of self-help: A suicide and self-harm prevention initiative within a prison setting, *Australian Psychologist, 37*, 237–244.

Hammett, T. H., Roberts, C., & Kennedy, S. (2001). Health-related issues in prisoner reentry. *Crime & Delinquency, 47*, 390–409.

Haney, C. (2003). The psychological impact of incarceration: Implications for post-prison adjustment. In J. Travis & M. Waul (Eds.), *Prisoners once removed: The impact of incarceration and re-entry on children, families, and communities* (pp. 33–66). Washington, DC: Urban Institute.

Haney, C. (2005). The contextual revolution in psychology and the question of prison effects. In A. Liebling & S. Maruna (Eds.), *The effects of imprisonment* (pp. 66–93). Cullompton, Devon, UK: Willan Publishing.

Harvey, J. (2011). Acknowledging and understanding complexity when providing therapy in prisons. *European Journal of Psychotherapy and Counselling, 13*, 303–315.

Harvey, J., & Smedley, K. (2010). *Psychological therapy in prisons and other secure settings*. Cullompton, Devon, UK: Willan Publishing.

Hayes, L.M. (1993). Suicidal or manipulative: Does it really matter? *Crisis: Journal of Crisis Intervention and Suicide Prevention, 14*, 154–156.

Holmes, G. (2010). *Psychology in the real world: Community based groupwork.* Ross on Wye, UK: PCCS Books.

Lane, C., Goldstein, N.E.S., Heilbrun, K., Cruise, K.R., & Pennacchia, D. (2012). Obstacles to research in residential juvenile justice facilities: Recommendations for researchers. *Behavioral Sciences and the Law, 30*, 49–68.

Liebling, A. (2004). *Prisons and their moral performance: A study of values, quality, and prison life*. Oxford, UK: Clarendon Press.

Maxfield, M., & Segal, D. (2008). Psychotherapy in non-traditional settings: A case of in-home cognitive-behavioral therapy with a depressed older adult. *Clinical Case Studies, 7*, 154–166.

McCorkle, R.C. (1992). Personal precautions to violence in prison. *Criminal Justice and Behavior, 19*, 160–173.

McMurran, M. (2002). *Motivating offenders to change: A guide to enhancing engagement in therapy*. Chichester, UK: Wiley.

Miller, W.R., & Rollnick, S. (2002). *Motivational interviewing: Preparing people for change* (2nd ed.). New York, NY: Guilford Press.

Mulcahy, C.A., Krezmien, M.P., Leone, P.E., Houchins, D.E., & Baltodano, H. (2008). Lessons learned: Barriers and solutions for conducting reading investigations in juvenile corrections settings. *Reading & Writing Quarterly: Overcoming Learning Difficulties, 24*, 239–252.

Pratt, D., Tarrier, N., Dunn, G., Awenat, Y., Shaw, J., Ulph, F., & Gooding, P. (in press). Cognitive behavioural suicide prevention for male prisoners: A pilot randomised controlled trial. *Psychological Medicine*.

Rollnick, S., Miller, W.R., & Butler, C.C. (2008). *Motivational interviewing in health care*. New York, NY: Guilford Press.

Smedley, K. (2010). Cognitive behaviour therapy with adolescents in secure settings. In J. Harvey & K. Smedley (Eds.), *Psychological therapy in prisons and other secure settings* (pp. 71–101). Cullompton, Devon, UK: Willan Publishing.

Toch, H. (1975). *Men in crisis: Human breakdowns in prison.* Chicago, IL: Aldine.

Toch, H. (1977). *Living in prison: The ecology of survival.* New York, NY: Free Press.

US Department of Health and Human Services. (2001). *National strategy for suicide prevention: Goals and objectives for action.* Rockville, MD: Public Health Service.

8 Improving the delivery of psychological therapy within a male high-security prison

A qualitative enquiry

Fiona Ulph

Background to empirical work

The empirical work presented in this chapter represents work conducted as part of a larger feasibility trial regarding researching the implementation of therapy for suicidal prisoners (Prevention of Suicide in Prisons Study; PROSPeR). The original design was constructed by an expert in prison research and a qualitative methods expert. There were two parts to the qualitative design: a feasibility study and an evaluation study. The feasibility study was an initial qualitative work package that planned to examine with prisoners and prison staff how best to implement the therapy within the prison, whilst the evaluation study was to collect preliminary data on the potential efficacy of the therapy for suicidal prisoners. This chapter focuses on the feasibility study. The design was reviewed as part of the grant application and feedback specifically mentioned the merits of the qualitative design. A highly competent researcher was employed and trained to conduct the qualitative research. Upon reviewing the data it became clear, however, that these data could not be used, raising the question of what had gone so wrong, that had been failed to be picked up through the design, review and training stages? We therefore designed a second study to enable us to learn from this setting.

A study was designed that focused on the following questions:

- What is the best way to recruit participants into research?
- How can usual ethical/research procedures be followed during the study within the constraints of the prison context?
- How do we manage participants exiting the study?

This time we designed the study into three phases. First, ex-offenders from the study's Service User Reference Group (SURG; see Chapter 6) were invited to participate in a focus group. These participants represented

116 *Fiona Ulph*

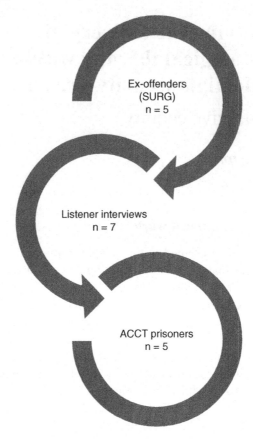

Figure 8.1 Three groups of participants contributing to the qualitative investigation

'experts' in that they had a lived experience of the prison setting, but also had received some research training and had vicarious research experience through their advisory roles. Secondly, Listener prisoners were interviewed. Within the English Prison system, prisoners can volunteer to become 'Listeners'. If successful, they receive training in sympathetic listening and befriending from the Samaritans, a UK-based organization that specializes in providing a listening service for people in distress. These represented people who not only had a current lived experience of the prison environment, but also were likely to have some insight into how best to work with prisoners who were the focus of this study – namely suicidal prisoners. They were also more likely to have a broad view of prison life given their role as the 'go-to' person for prisoners. Further, they were likely to be able to convey insightful views in an interview setting and be prepared to interact with outside researchers given their role and the training they would have received. Finally, prisoners who were currently known to be suicidal were interviewed. These were the prisoners who were the target of this research project. By interviewing them last we could apply research advice from the previous phases; this also enabled us to test out ideas with prisoners who may potentially be reluctant to engage at length with research teams.

Data collection and analysis were iterative, with data analysis in previous phases informing data collection in later phases. For example the data from the ex-offender focus group were analysed and fed into the Listener interviews. Thematic analysis was used (Boyatzis, 1998) and a deductive theme structure was applied to the data as the team were interested in key phases in the research cycle – recruitment into the study and engagement during the study. Data were analysed at a manifest level. Once data had been organized into this structure an inductive analysis was conducted. This approach of combining both deductive and inductive thematic analyses has previously been cited as a rigorous approach in qualitative design (Fereday & Muir-Cochrane, 2006). At all stages findings are placed in the context of the wider literature.

Recruitment into studies

Lobmaier, Kunoe, and Waal (2010) conducted a randomised control trial (RCT) examining treatment for opioid dependence. Potential participants were given study information via information folders distributed onto the wings. Prisoners could then refer themselves into the study via phone or be referred by staff. In this way, prison staff were asked to help identify potential participants. Once prisoners who were interested in participating had been put in touch with the research team, they received consent forms and an information sheet. Within this study, 1,500 information leaflets were distributed. From this intensive recruitment activity, they report they had *no* prisoners who self-referred. Prison staff referred 172 prisoners, but when the research team contacted them 100 of these prisoners either stated that they did not use drugs or refused to participate. Thus from the original 172, only 46 prisoners consented. At six-month follow-up, only 26 prisoners remained in the sample. The authors themselves state "Despite intensive efforts of criminal justice authorities, prison staff and researchers [. . .] resulted in small and selected sample" (p. 7) and cite other RCTs that had been discontinued because of sample issues (Shearer, Wodak, & Dolan, 2007).

Thus prisoners may be difficult to reach with the study information distribution routes conventionally used in research. The authors of this chapter suggest that other key barriers are low motivation of prisoners to participate and issues of dealing with early release of prisoners. Indeed, Patenaude and Laufersweiler-Dwyer (2001) concluded that conducting research with prisoners is difficult and complicated. This is partly attributed to the fact that not only prisoners, but also staff are seen as distrusting researchers (Patenaude, 2004). It is crucial to acknowledge that prisoners have it within their power to, in essence, halt research through their disengagement if they do not want it to succeed. Although it could be argued that this is true of any research project in any setting, it is usually only 'gatekeepers' who really have this power as participants are dispersed. Within a prison setting where research participants are within a closed society, the power of key individuals to generate uniform rejection behaviours is much stronger.

Other issues that have been highlighted as creating barriers to participation in research include researchers using common words such as 'informant' that may not be suitable in a prison setting, as they have another meaning (Patenaude, 2004). What is striking in the aforementioned literature is that although it is acknowledged that research challenges derive from establishing good relationships with prisoners, none of this literature included the views of prisoners about how to best address these issues.

A common strategy to work in settings where it may be challenging to engage participants is to seek out guidelines regarding how best to conduct such research. However, there is a recognised lack of guidelines for prisoner research (Fox, Zambrana, & Lane, 2010), and existing guidance focuses either on fairly standard methods practice rather than how to operationalise this in the prison context per se (Megargee, 1995) or on how to gain access without addressing how to conduct the research subsequently (Marquart, 1986). Without acknowledgement that researchers are working in a different environment in which standard research practices may be ineffective, there is the risk that researchers continue to run effective research projects.

One piece of guidance that could be gleaned was the importance of building respect and communication between researchers and staff (Lane, Turner, & Flores, 2004). A reflective piece regarding conducting quantitative surveys in a prison setting, (Fox et al., 2010) suggested the following lessons for researchers: read documents out loud in recognition of literacy issues, maintain a friendly and respectful relationship with staff (e.g. Lane et al., 2004; Reback, Cohen, Freese, & Shoptaw, 2002), dress in business attire, allow additional time for every research task in recognition of the prison system, ensure that you are friendly, yet respected by prisoners. Fox et al. (2010) suggested that low response rates should be expected and recognise that some of their potential solutions to this problem are ethically dubious. What is striking again is that the prisoners' voices are missing from this work. What is also concerning is that the study design used in this publication would not be suitable for most RCTs, as within this study mass questionnaire completion was used in one sitting (i.e. numerous prisoners were brought into a room together and asked to complete a questionnaire once). If, with such a design, there are still recruitment issues despite a heavy investment in trying to facilitate recruitment, this calls to question the feasibility of conducting RCTs, which require a researcher to work one-on-one with prisoners, often completing multiple scales at numerous time points.

In a more recent study, Eldridge, Robinson, Corey, Brems, and Johnson (2012) sought to identify what constituted the most important ethical issue when conducting prison research. The context of this question was conducting HIV/AIDS research in the prison setting. Although 92 participants were included in this study, they were all professionals and no prisoners were asked. Although important issues were highlighted such as confidentiality and privacy, autonomy and informed consent and justice and access, the authors raised problems rather than provided potential solutions. Thus researchers seeking guidance regarding how best to conduct successful robust research in the prison setting have little guidance.

Prisoners' views regarding research conduct

Participants in our study had clear ideas about how best to conduct research within the prison setting.

Recruitment

A major issue discussed focused on recruitment of participants and how best practice could be developed to ensure targets could be met. It became clear through listening to prisoners that the conventional practice of accessing participants via gatekeepers would be hugely detrimental in this setting and, rather, a community engagement approach was needed.

> Whoever is in there as a part of and doing the research if they are seen talking to screws then they are compromising themselves, because people will turn around and say anything you say to them will go straight to the screws.
>
> (SURG focus group, Male #1)

Other conventional means of publicizing research were raised and discussed, including posters and newspapers. What was of interest is how participants appeared to feel that the most effective ways of recruiting participants would be via prisoner-specific modes of information such as the prisoner newspaper, television or the 'prison information network'. This informal information network is simply prisoners talking to other prisoners, but it became clear that this was a key way in which information was gathered in prisons and importantly was a source that prisoners would trust:

> So the best people to get it out there are prisoners themselves to pass on the information and let other prisoners know.
>
> (SURG focus group, Female #1)

One suggestion from the Listener interviews was to use them:

> The thing is to make people aware and not make them frightened, now this could be spread via the listening scheme because honestly speaking you will be amazed by how many people approach Listeners with nothing to do with listening just purely and simply as a mine of information because they think know we know everything, [yeah] we don't necessarily know everything but we do say we will find out for people if they want information.
>
> (Listener #3)

Other suggestions included using key times in the prison system such as induction, when a prisoner first arrives at the prison, to provide information. For example putting information in induction packs was often suggested, because this is a time when prisoners are already seeking information and are more likely to attend to the information they are given.

The participants also made it clear that conventional means of identifying eligible participants is highly problematic in this setting. Participants discussed the need to not show weakness and the powerful impact labels assigned to participants could have on their welfare:

> [. . .] If you target the vulnerable you won't get them all. It won't work in jail, you have to target the issue not because they are vulnerable or not, not just because they are going to be bullied or shagged or whatever, [everyone laughs] yeah, but you're putting the stamp on them already they are not worth shit if it's only for the vulnerable [. . .] you're like making people like "oi clean my pad you vulnerable little bastard" because if someone got hold of that on the landings they will use it.
>
> (SURG focus group, Male #2)

This issue of having to be careful about showing weakness also came up when discussing how to provide prisoners with information and was given as a reason why researchers should try to meet with prisoners individually to brief them about research:

> Also bear in mind a lot of these people are on medication and they are not playing with a full deck and they will give the impression that they understand when they don't when they are in a group setting but in a one to one basis they would probably tell you and ask for you to repeat it and ask you to explain further.
>
> (Listener #3)

It also became clear that within this setting all behaviours came at a price (such as reading/writing other people's letters) and anything that could be used as currency could be a massive advantage for a prisoner. Therefore, although it was explained that some prisoners would elect to have another prisoner read the study information sheet for them as a means of illiterate prisoners gaining access to information, it was suggested that researchers should be aware of this 'cost' for a prisoner when designing studies. Linked to this need to be aware of the 'prison economy' was the warning that researchers must carefully think through the use of incentives, as some prisoners would play act the part of an eligible participant to access the incentives because they could be valuable currency. Thus without sufficient awareness of the setting, researchers may not understand that key participants may not be able to access studies without a 'cost' and that some eager participants may not be suitable for the study:

> *Male #2:* The negatives is [sic] that you are offering carrots for somebody like monkeys wanting peanuts you have to get somebody who is interesting in what you are doing.
>
> *Male #1:* Yeah if you give too much then you will [get] folk coming along for what they can get out of it more rather than
>
> [. . .]
>
> *Male #2:* Yeah I was given information for months and I got stuff every time I went in do you know what I mean? I would read a book and tell them what they wanted to hear.
>
> *Male #1:* If there was a good screw you were on a couple of mars bars and whatever everyone would be bloody suicidal.
>
> (SURG focus group)

The issue of how incentives may make it difficult for prisoners to refuse participation (for example if they really needed the currency) is raised in Eldridge et al. (2012). The aforementioned data show how data integrity may be jeopardised by incentives, whilst the following data show how incentives can have a wider ranging destabilising influence in the prison:

> *Male #1:*   Yeah but then all them gifts become bribery, if you not getting the gifts you can sell them there and all of a sudden there become a whole load of barons on the wing, get a half ounce for that pen you have got from them.
>
> *Researcher:*   So what have we started all over our pens?
> *Male #1:*   You have got to look at the spin off all the gifts.
> *Male #2:*   Everything has value.
> *Male #1:*   Sometimes it can do more damage than good.
>
> (SURG focus group)

Similar to community healthcare research, the power of the researcher 'being available' was extremely strong. Participants advised that researchers needed to be regularly physically present in prisons and efforts should be made to break down the sense of 'them' and 'us' that is pervasive in prisons. This led to a discussion around 'taking the white coat off':

> *Male #2:*   You have to like you say specify why you are doing it and what for, you have to make it clear and you have to like take that white coat off it and say listen this is for everybody.
>
> *Researcher:*   So when you say take the white coat off . . .
> *Male #2:*   Yeah take the paperwork out of it be human with it, be real, be there.
> *Female #1:*   Be real otherwise people just dint [sic] want to know.
>
> (SURG focus group)

This led to further descriptions that highlight that any outsider seen in a prison setting is evaluated and judged by prisoners:

> *Male #1:*   Yeah it's like you have got your screws with the uniform and then you have got other people that come in 'the suits' now the suits are the same as the screws they are like screws without uniforms.
>
> *Female #1:*   Officer no keys.
>
> (SURG focus group)

Thus anything that enabled the potential participants to 'suss out' the researcher, even if it was vicariously via televised interviews, was seen as beneficial.

> You should have something in research that if you're doing this research you need get yourself known on the landings even before you put pen to paper. Do you know what I mean? You have been there and you have an office there and then people start noticing you and talking to you and they know you are not involved in, you know you're saying you will do this and you stop doing that, because you're not. You are there to help before you even sign anything.
>
> (SURG focus group, Male #2)

This fitted with a similar suggestion from the listeners about how information could be spread about the studies:

> You could have focus groups you know could come down to the wing and have a chat to the prisoners and tell them yourselves if you had the time to do it that you could let them all know before hand when you are going to be there and give an evening or afternoon to chat to them about it that would be an idea.
>
> (Listener #3)

The benefits of establishing rapport with participants through informal conversations and trying to treat prisoners as ' individual human beings' was also noted by (Quina et al., 2008), who describe how it can ensure that the research data are meaningfully contextualised.

Engagement during the study

One of the most fundamental practices within research is the process of gaining informed consent. Within most research settings this would entail a participant signing a consent form. Although it is common practice for participants to keep a copy of a signed consent form, there were concerns from the team that this could compromise confidentiality in a setting such as a prison where there is no privacy. The prisoners' simple solution to this which was just to ask the prisoners whether they felt they wanted a copy. There were some who felt that they would like a copy and would simply leave it with their personal possessions in their pad and this would not be a problem as prisoners respect that, others who said they would advise any prisoner against holding confidential information, whilst another explained it was actually the staff they would be more concerned about maintaining secrecy from:

> I wouldn't [keep the form] in prison because at the end of the day staff can go through your property in your cell so just say to them if you ever want to look at them [the consent forms] you can, we will show them, but no normally people don't keep anything because the rules of the prison are that they can come and check your cell at any time so for confidentiality no don't keep anything.
>
> (Listener #7)

So one solution offered by the prisoners was for the researchers to keep their copy centrally, but in a way that the prisoner could access if necessary. Another reason for prisoners not accepting paperwork was that prisoners could have a different view of paperwork:

> *P:*   Yeah, I mean you can keep any paperwork really. You can keep all your legal paperwork and everything else. People probably wouldn't tend to keep a copy anyway.
> *Researcher:* Why is that?
> *P:*   I don't know, I suppose it's people in prison, isn't it? They're just . . . paperwork, I don't need that. They don't see it as important.
>
> (ACCT #2)

This illustrates the need to understand the viewpoint of prisoners before interpreting behaviour. The need to understand the prison environment became even more stark when discussing how best to conduct research in this setting. It became clear that some standard practices in community research could have devastating effects in this setting. For example it is standard that participants in the community should be facilitated to engage with research in a way that their participation remains confidential (with the exception of relevant health professionals). Participants in this study intimated that this practice could put the participant at grave risk, as nothing within prison was a secret and any behaviour to try and keep secrets may cause prisoners to become targets.

> *Researcher:* One of things [ethics committees] will say we want these people to take part without other people knowing about it, so from what you are saying we need to go back to ethics and go forget that.

Male #2:	Oh you will get them killed you can't hide it you see you can't hide it.
Male #1:	You can't have secrets.
Female #3:	Try and hide it and they will think you are up to something else.

[Laughter]

| *Researcher:* | So we would make it worse? |
| *Male #2:* | A hateful word in prison is a grass, if you do that they will think you're a grass and that's you dead you're on the protection wing then if you put that doubt in somebody's mind then you are gone. |

(SURG focus group)

Another example of where practice would need to be modified was in the provision of study documentation. It is most common that researchers will provide written information sheets and require signed consent forms. Yet it was repeatedly emphasized how low literacy rates are within prisons. Thus relying on such written information may inadvertently skew samples to those who can read, or those who can afford to 'pay' other prisoners to read for them or were prepared to use 'wing insiders' to help with their paperwork, highlighting further the need for researchers to engage with prisoners directly to ensure all are facilitated to participate. Although this challenge is also noted in Eldridge et al. (2012), no potential solutions are provided.

Another example of where common research practice could be hugely detrimental was in how to handle situations where appointments with participants could not be honored. Numerous barriers to maintaining contact with participants in prisons were acknowledged, yet a type of dependency was discussed whereby if contact that was promised was not honored this could easily trigger a prisoner to either disengage from the research or become aggressive. One of the key quotes from the study came from an answer to the question of what would make for a good researcher: "Who are there for you as much as you are for them" (ACCT #1). Looking into the data, it became clear just how much prisoners invested into participating in research. Prisoners would describe how the journey to the researcher's office in the prison could take hours, just so they could come and see the researcher for 20 minutes. The participants had to accept that other prisoners and staff would know what they were doing, with the potential aforementioned consequences, and they may also have had to give up some paid work in order to participate. Thus, although they acknowledged there were numerous reasons why a prisoner may not be able to hold an appointment with a researcher, and vice versa, it is important that the researcher recognizes how much the prisoner is 'investing' into this project. Therefore, not letting that prisoner know directly why the session would not go ahead was seen as disrespectful and a huge let down:

Male #2:	You're in a place where if you break that [trust] I am in a place that's shut down and I will knock the crap out of him next door because you let me down, the consequences of what you can do to somebody determine their life in that jail you have to think about that.
Male #1:	For some people getting involved in the study and having that session to look forward to will become their focus because they will have nothing else you know some people are not getting [a] letter or getting phone calls they are getting bugger all. The study will become everything to them so if they are looking forward to going down on Thursday seeing [name of researcher] or whatever and it doesn't happen then that guy's world is going to crash and burn.
Female #1:	Then you have to start all over again the trust is gone that's it.

(SURG focus group)

Part of the reasoning for this may be found in the statement from a Listener that "the system is designed to keep everyone unsure and confused you have to bear that in mind" (Listener #3). Inherent in this is that by leaving the participant in this state the researcher may be seen as becoming part of the system, or may simply be the tipping point for a person who is under huge amounts of stress. This highlighted how carefully the relationship between participants and researchers needed to be handled and recognized that in order to engage in any type of research, prisoners are placing a huge amount of trust in researchers, which makes them potentially vulnerable.

The key to managing this and all other barriers to conventional research practice appeared to be from ensuring that researchers were clear and honest about the research process and how it would work in this setting from the outset. If prisoners were let down by researchers, it became clear how quickly the study would effectively be shut down via disengagement from prisoners. This highlighted further the need for researchers to truly understand the environment they are operating in so that they are able to provide realistic expectations to prisoners.

One of the key reasons why the original qualitative data were unsuitable for use was that in practice the ability to conduct semi-structured interviews in a prison setting was affected by the reality of prison life. For example the research staff had little control over whether or when the prisoners would be available, and the time with the prisoners was often cut short by a need to return the prisoners back to their residential wings or by prison 'lockdowns' (security-imposed restrictions of personnel movements to ascertain the precise whereabouts of all prisoners). One of the key challenges for our research design, therefore, was how to establish sufficient rapport with prisoners to enable interviews to flow quickly and yet achieve depth. Although this specific issue may not be relevant to quantitative RCT designs, the underlying issue of how to establish quick, meaningful and honest dialogue with a participant is crucially important to the engagement of the participant in the study and the veracity of the data. When asked how best researchers could facilitate communication with prison participants, key themes were control, honesty and trust. Indeed, one ACCT prisoner summed it up as needing to be "Open, honest, down to earth" (ACCT#3).

Although it may at first appear difficult to give a prisoner control, the participants highlighted subtle ways this could be done, which included the decision about whether they kept the consent form and decisions about whether they wanted further support:

> Yeah, are you okay? Do you want us to let anybody know? Then you can give the option; do you want to let staff know you're a bit down or do you want us to let a Listener know?
>
> (ACCT #2)

Another participant explained how simply giving prisoners some choice over when they are seen could be a novel experience for them:

> [. . .] you can give them the option as to when else to see them. And if they could pick a range of hours between, say 10 and 4, or 10 and 2, then they think they're making the appointment, not you.
>
> (ACCT #1)

Part of the need for this was down to how prisoners experience 'the system' (i.e. the prison), and inherent in this was the need to be seen as not being part of that system:

> [. . .] just be honest because this is all prisoners want honesty because they don't get honesty from the system.
>
> (Listener #3)

P:	Well, it comes down to trust on both sides.
Researcher:	Yeah. Tell me how we can gain someone's trust in a small space of time?
P:	Be more open.
Researcher:	Okay. In what way, how could we be more open?
P:	When you've done the explaining, to actually talk to the person not as a prisoner, but as a person. And there are a lot in here that talk down to you as if you're nothing.

(ACCT #4)

One factor that researchers would need to accept is that developing trust may take a lot of time and multiple visits for prisoners, and this should to be factored into the research design before the important data are collected to ensure that meaningful data are achieved.

Exiting research

A standard process in research is to provide participants with copies of the results, but there were concerns in the team that this could compromise prisoners. The prisoners had mixed feelings on this. Some felt that it would be a way for the team to show it really had listened to the prisoners, whilst others thought there may be generic interest in the results:

[. . .] there are people who would be interested [laughs] some boring people might enjoy the presentation they probably like it when you stand up and present it all [laughs]. I am kidding. In prison a lot of people are interested in psychology in general they do like it they like learning about things. I am sure there will be people in prison who will be interested in reading it.

(Listener #1)

A suggestion made in the focus group, which was then developed in the interviews, was to provide people with certificates:

It's daft to say, but things like getting a certificate that gives a lot a credit that they have done something and they got something out of it at the end. Also tell them there is support after it if they need, it doesn't stop here.

(Listener #7)

Well, a lot of people in prison have not been to school; they've got no certificates or anything. There's one lad on our wing, he's doing [name of course], he got a certificate and he was over the moon, he was ecstatic, he goes the first certificate I've ever had! So yeah, certificates for anything. I mean I've got about 20 certificates here, so.

(ACCT #2)

Another issue in closing a study is how participants can contact the research team in the future. A setting such as a prison where contact is largely reliant on a researcher being in the prison makes this situation problematic. One suggestion was that prisoners were left with a telephone number:

[. . .] you've got a phone number sorted out; that would be a lot easier. I would definitely phone. When I first saw it, I thought about it but the phone would; yeah, I'd give them a ring.

(ACCT #1)

However, there were several concerns raised about this method of communication, including that phone conversations are rarely confidential and would cost the prisoner time (when they could be talking to family or others) and money, both of which are precious. Another suggestion that would work during the duration of the research study was that the study could set up its own 'app', which is the system prisoners use to request access to services such as healthcare and so on. Through this system, prisoners could request a meeting with the research team if they had concerns, wanted to withdraw and so on. Problems linked to this system included issues such as the length of time it took for apps to be granted and concerns that they were not confidential and could go missing. Another solution mooted for the end of the study was that prisoners are given contact details of other services/organisations that were still routinely in, or accessible whilst in, prison:

P:	You can just erm just drop a line with contact details and send them other organisations that can offer the support they need and tell them we have finished our part with you, but we care so here are other people that may be able to support you
Researcher:	Yeah so you think advising them of other support available would be helpful?
P:	Yeah definitely don't just leave it.

(Listener #7)

A repeated response was that whatever the researchers had set up in terms of contacting the team, exiting the research or the study shutting down, it was crucial that this was all made clear to the prisoners beforehand. Once again, this appears to feed into the idea of needing to be honest, giving the prisoners a sense of what to expect, and being seen as different from their usual experiences with the system.

Implications for research practice

Some of the key issues researchers, ethical review boards and funders need to be aware of when planning and approving research in this setting are as follows:

1   Standard research practices may cause more harm than good within this setting.
2   It is vital that researchers fully understand the environment they are working within in order to conduct ethical research. As such, time should be factored into designs for researchers to spend time acquainting themselves with the prison setting, and participant and public involvement should be seen as a necessary safeguard, not a luxury.
3   Resources need to be provided to enable researchers to 'become known' to prisoners for effective, valid research to be conducted, such as being interviewed by the prison newspaper or spending time on wings.

It is understandable that the literature regarding conducting research in prisons may cause funders and researchers to question whether robust research is feasible within this setting. The answer to this question appears to be 'yes', so long as sufficient consideration is taken of the adjustments that need to be made. Indeed, to ensure that this is done correctly, one of the simplest solutions is to talk to prisoners. The participants within our study came up with good, feasible ideas without any nonsense, highlighting vital safety and ethical issues that the researchers on our team were not aware of despite being experienced researchers. It is also of concern that mapping the literature suggestions onto what the prisoners were saying highlights how some of the current suggestion in the literature could cause more harm than good and may indeed be creating some of the barriers between researchers and their participants that we are seeking to break down. Having initial 'design' meetings with invested prisoners does not need to be resource intensive and is likely to be hugely instrumental in ensuring that research studies are successful in recruiting, but more important that they are run safely and gain robust data from the relevant participants. They should be seen as being key in ensuring that the first ethical dictum of 'first, do no harm' is met. Furthermore, simply the act of talking to prisoners as a preliminary step means that the research team is already halfway there to removing the white coat.

References

Boyatzis, R. E. (1998). *Transforming qualitative information: Thematic analysis and code development.* Thousand Oaks, CA: Sage.

Eldridge, G. D., Robinson, V. R., Corey, S., Brems, C., & Johnson, M. E. (2012). Ethical challenges in conducting HIV/AIDS research in correctional settings. *Journal of Correctional Health Care, 18*, 309–318.

Fereday, J., & Muir-Cochrane, E. (2006). Demonstrating rigor using thematic analysis: A hybrid approach of inductive and deductive coding and theme development. *International Journal of Qualitative Methods, 5*(1), 1–11.

Fox, K., Zambrana, K., & Lane, J. (2010). Getting in (and staying in) when everyone else wants to get out: 10 lessons learned from conducting research with inmates. *Journal of Criminal Justice Education, 22*(2), 304–327.

Lane, J., Turner, S., & Flores, C. (2004). Researcher-practitioner collaboration in corrections: Overcoming hurdles for successful partnerships. *Criminal Justice Review 29*(1), 97–114.

Lobmaier, P. P., Kunoe, N., & Waal, H. (2010). Treatment research in prison: Problems and solutions in a randomised trial. *Addiction Research and Theory, 18*(1), 1–13.

Marquart, J. W. (1986). Doing research in prison: The strengths and weaknesses of full participation as a guard. *Justice Quarterly, 3*(1), 15–32.

Megargee, E. I. (1995). Assessment research in correctional settings: Methodological issues and practical problems. *Psychological Assessment, 7*(3), 359–366.

Patenaude, A. (2004). No promises, but I'm wiling to listen and tell what I hear: Conducting qualitative research among prison inmates and staff. *The Prison Journal, 84*, 69S–91S.

Patenaude, A. L., & Laufersweiler-Dwyer, D. (2001). *Arkansas comprehensive substance abuse treatment program: Process evaluation of the modified therapeautic community.* Washington, DC: National Institute of Justice.

Quina, K., Garis, A. V., Stevenson, J., Garrido, M., Brown, J., Richman, R., & Mitchell, K. (2008). Through the bullet-proof glass: Conducting research in prison settings. *Journal of Trauma & Dissociation, 8*(2), 123–139.

Reback, C. J., Cohen, A. J., Freese, T. E., & Shoptaw, S. (2002). Making collaborations work: Key components of practice/research partnerships. *Journal of Drug Issues, 32*(3), 837–848.

Shearer, J., Wodak, A. D., & Dolan, K. A. (2007). Evaluation of a prison-based naltrexone program. *International Journal of Prisoner Health, 3*, 214–224.

9   Concluding reflections

Daniel Pratt

Summary and conclusions

Mental health problems are significantly more prevalent amongst prisoners than the general community, with as many as 9 out of every 10 prisoners in the UK experiencing one or more mental disorders (Department of Health, 2001; Earthrowl, O'Grady, & Birmingham, 2003; Singleton, Meltzer, & Gatward, 1998). Furthermore, co-morbidity rates are substantial, with 1 in 7 prisoners experiencing more than four concurrent psychiatric disorders (Singleton et al., 1998).

The last decade has witnessed an increasing role for the NHS in the provision of healthcare within prisons (Department of Health & HM Prison Service, 2002). Prisoners are entitled to access the same quality and range of health services that would be available to them within the community. However, this principle of 'equivalence' has revealed the problems facing prison mental healthcare services who routinely work with offenders and prisoners who can often present with a complex combination of problems related to mental health, substance use and personality disorder in addition to other social issues. Whilst the prison environment and experience of daily life inside prison can be seriously detrimental to mental health and well-being, the identification of prisoners experiencing mental distress is ineffective. Prisoners' mental health problems are left both undetected and untreated (Birmingham, 2003). The provision of suitable and effective mental health services to prisoners can be challenging because the prison environment and regime are not specifically designed to be therapeutic, rather more focused upon discipline and control (Hughes, 2000).

Although significant improvements have made to the delivery of mental health services within prisons following the publication of the influential Bradley Report (Department of Health, 2009), one particular issue that continues to cause concern is the high prevalence of suicidal behaviour in prison in comparison with the general population (HM Inspectorate of

Prisons, 2014; Travis, 2015). For every suicide attempt, there is also considerable 'collateral damage', with conservative estimates suggesting each attempt leaves at least six survivors with a profound and lasting emotional effect. Family, friends and prison and health service professionals may feel guilt, shame and remorse and remain especially anxious and concerned about the risk of further suicidal behaviour and about their responsibilities in trying to prevent further suicide attempts. For some, this damage may be long lasting, and the person's life may never be the same again.

Prisoners and their families are a significant part of the socially excluded population, often coming from marginalised populations that have poor access to healthcare in the community. Because the vast majority of prisoners return to the community, periods of incarceration offer important opportunities for a variety of prevention and treatment interventions. Indeed, national and international policies emphasise imprisonment as a rare opportunity to address the pre-existing unmet health needs of a 'hard-to-reach' sector of society (Department of Health & HM Prison Service, 2002; World Health Organization, 2014) and the need to improve access to mental health treatments for offenders, including interventions to reduce the risk of suicidal behaviour (Department of Health, 2013). Taking advantage of these important opportunities stands to benefit not only the prisoners themselves, their families, partners, and friends, but also the larger public health arena as well as producing downstream savings in other publicly funded services (Hammett, Gaiter, & Crawford, 1998).

Prisoners have been identified as a high-risk group in the Suicide Prevention Strategies for England (Department of Health, 2002; 2012). However, there are no evidence-based psychological interventions to prevent suicide amongst this group. In this monograph, we have presented a range of ideas, propositions, summaries of evidence and reflections from completed and on-going research studies. This material has resulted from a decade of clinical research into suicidal behaviour amongst individuals incarcerated within a prison setting. An argument has been proposed that a population-level epidemiological approach to the understanding of prison suicide alone is insufficient and that a psychological formulation at an individual level is also warranted if we are to deliver interventions that reduce the likelihood and incidence of suicidal behaviour. For such a formulation to be possible, there is a need to develop a deeper understanding of the psychology of the suicidal prisoner. What motivates the suicidal prisoner to desire his or her own death? In what ways does he or she differ and match the suicidal individual living in the community? How should we extend the current psychological theories and models of the suicidal individual living at home to those incarcerated?

This research aims to highlight the limited knowledge we have about the psychological mechanisms, and how they interact, upon which we would base our formulation of the suicidal prisoner. We strongly hold the view that by concurrently developing psychological theory and practice in equal measure, we are better able to deliver informed interventions that target the specific mechanisms leading to suicidal behaviour. We have previously argued that there may be a number of psychological mechanisms that underlies suicidal behaviour (Tarrier et al., 2013). Perhaps mechanisms are specific to psychiatric diagnostic groups (e.g. depression, schizophrenia, PTSD), or there may be trans-diagnostic mechanisms that operate irrespective of diagnosis, or there may be a common mechanism that co-occurs with psychiatric diagnoses (e.g. hopelessness). We may also now have to consider iatrogenic mechanisms associated with context and environment (e.g. prisons, forensic psychiatric services). Furthermore, we have to remain open to a complex interaction between specific, common and iatrogenic mechanisms. Hence, the need for a clearer understanding of such mechanisms is apparent even though this may not be an easy need to meet!

We have seen that psychological research conducted within the constraints of the prison environment is not without its challenges and frustrations. Many of the 'rules of engagement' that experienced researchers will be familiar with from community studies cannot be imported simply into the prison setting, if we are to gather truly meaningful data. The subtleties of the various prison cultures and customs, amongst both staff and offenders, need to remain in the forefront of the researcher's mind. Standard research practices have to be amended to allow for the necessary restrictions of the prison regime. Prisoners' motivation to engage and contribute to this research agenda should not be assumed. With such little control within their daily lives, the voluntary participation in a research study may provide a limited opportunity to exert some influence over prisoners' activity. As for so many aspects of prisoners' daily life, the potential participant's availability for the research study is not entirely within his or her own control. Non-attendance at research appointments, curtailed interview duration, contextual distractions and impoverished environments may be likely for the prison-based researcher who is tasked with the job of working around such potential barriers. Creativity, ingenuity, perseverance and tolerance are absolute necessities for the researcher to become successful! Notwithstanding such difficulties, good quality research can be conducted.

Within this book, we have also seen the emerging findings and reflections of two recent investigations that endeavoured to assess the feasibility of delivering preventative, psychological interventions to individual prisoners identified to be at risk of suicidal behaviour. Of note is that both interventions are informed by a cognitive behavioural approach. This may be less surprising when one considers the evidence base for prisoner interventions, which has consistently highlighted the positive effects of cognitive behavioural interventions for treating offending behaviour (Lipsey, Landenberger, & Wilson, 2007; McDougall, Perry, Clarbour, Bowles, & Worthy, 2009; Wilson, Bouffard, & Mackenzie, 2005).

Cognitive behavioural interventions targeting offending behaviours have tended to focus upon (i) cognitive restructuring or thought challenging, (ii) developing new and enhancing existing coping skills, and (iii) interpersonal problem-solving training. These three techniques are all founded on the theory that cognition affects behaviour such that changes in behaviour result from changes in cognitions. Dobson & Khatri (2000) highlighted the common feature of these interventions is an emphasis on "demonstrable, behavioural outcomes achieved primarily through changes in the way an individual perceives, reflects upon, and, in general, thinks about their life circumstance" (p. 908). By supporting the prisoner to become more aware of his or her cognitive processes that lead to unhelpful or unwanted behaviours, changes become possible.

Because previous reviews have highlighted cognitive behavioural approaches to be the most effective approach within offending behaviour programmes, it is somewhat surprising that such approaches have not been extended to target other unwanted and unhelpful prisoner behaviours such as suicide and self-injury. Despite the exaggerated rates of prisoner suicide, perhaps this issue is less surprising when one considers the severely limited access to psychological interventions for other mental health problems experienced by prisoners (Department of Health, 2009). Nevertheless, this book has attempted to act as an impetus by providing preliminary evidence of the feasible and acceptable delivery of cognitive behaviour therapies for suicidal prisoners and the very real potential such interventions offer to the individual in reducing his or her suicidal behaviours.

Directions for future research

Theory developments

As highlighted in Chapter 2, the existent literature on prison suicide has been dominated by studies of the characteristics and correlates that surround prisoner deaths and the identification of high-risk groups. Only a minority of studies has attempted to understand the psychological underpinnings that cause individuals to attempt suicide whilst incarcerated. Of these investigations undertaken so far, the most frequently used methodology has been a cross-sectional assessment of psychological states using self-report measures completed by vulnerable individuals. However, retrospective methods are exposed to a range of biases such as distortions in memory, inaccurate recall, over-generalised memories, response bias, demand characteristics and so on. Furthermore, such methods do not allow for the assessment of fluctuation in the variable being assessed and the interacting relationship between variables. If we are to further our understanding of the psychological mechanisms that lead to the development and maintenance of suicidal ideation, we need to advance the research methodologies available for use within prisons (Felthous, 2011).

Experience sampling methodology (ESM) methods have enabled the measurement of psychological variables such as affects, cognitions and appraisals as they occur within the context of the participants' daily lives (Csikszentmihalyi & Larson, 1987). ESM methods enable an ecologically valid approach to the accurate capture of real-time experiences, especially affective and cognitive states (Palmier-Claus et al., 2011). Briefly, this method requires the participant to record a momentary assessment of his or her experiential state at several time points throughout the day. An electronic pager, programmable wristwatch or mobile phone may be used to signal to the participant, who then rates his or her experiential state, yielding up to 60 assessments during an average week.

This technique has been used across a range of different clinical populations and to investigate various psychological problems, although its use in prison settings is scarce. We have begun to amend the ESM method to be suitable for the prison setting, which has led to some interesting new understandings, For example we conducted an ESM study with suicidal prisoners to investigate the role of anger as a predictor of suicidal ideation and found anger to be significantly associated with concurrent high levels of suicidal ideation, yet anger at one time point did not predict suicidal ideation at the next time point (Humber, Emsley, Pratt, & Tarrier, 2013). The depth of detail offered by ESM is likely to lead to more nuanced and subtle understandings of the lived experience of suicide in prison; as such, this methodology offers an exciting opportunity.

Adverse childhood experiences have been shown to be associated with an increased risk of lifetime suicidal ideation (Afifi et al., 2008; Corcoran, Gallagher, Keeley, Arensman, & Perry, 2006; Dube et al., 2001). However, the potential impact of early life events and insecure attachments upon the future development of suicidality amongst prisoners is not well understood. Offenders constitute a group for which the experience of adversity is high, with most prisoners having experienced a relatively high degree of trauma during childhood and adolescence (Barton, Meade, Cumming, & Samuels, 2014; Godet-Mardirossian, Jehel, & Falissard, 2011). Anecdotally, from our own experiences of delivering cognitive behavioural therapy to suicidal prisoners, childhood adversity, especially physical or sexual abuse, contributed to the longitudinal formulation of the majority of cases. The psychological impact of such adverse events upon the prisoner's motivation for suicide tended to be understood within the context of insecure attachment and the development and maintenance of a now maladaptive internal working model for seeking and deserving help. A clearer understanding of this aspect of prisoner suicidality should be a target for future research.

Though early experiences and the security of attachments may act as contributory and precipitating factors to suicidality (de Jong, 1992; Lizardi et al., 2011), it seems unlikely that these factors alone would be sufficiently precise to identify individual prisoners at particularly high risk of suicide. As such, future investigations should also look to examine the intervening factors that mediate the relationship between early experiences and prisoner suicidality. Of relevance could be the role of situational and self-appraisals, such as defeat, entrapment and hopelessness, that are becoming established as key mediators amongst community samples. It may also prove important to examine factors that buffer the impact of negative life experiences, thus protecting the individual prisoner from suicidality.

There is also growing interest surrounding the role of emotional regulation and suicide, with some psychological theories proposing suicidal behaviour results from an individual's inability to tolerate or modulate his or her experience of negative emotions (Lynch, Cheavens, Morse, & Rosenthal, 2004). The inversed argument has also been made within the 'resilience' literature within positive psychology; that is those individuals who are better at perceiving, integrating, understanding and managing their emotions would be less likely to engage in suicidal behaviour (Cha & Nock, 2009). This approach has proposed emotional intelligence may play a protective role against suicide (Ciarrochi, Deane, & Anderson, 2002). The role of emotional regulation amongst prisoners engaging in self-injurious behaviours has tended to be limited to those inmates attracting a label of borderline personality disorder, which is not surprising because being prone to strong emotions, mood swings and feelings that are difficult to cope with are key features of these diagnoses. Nevertheless, the likely presence of emotional regulation difficulties amongst suicidal prisoners without such diagnoses highlights the need to broaden our understanding of how enhancing emotional regulation skills or emotional intelligence may, more generally, contribute to the prevention of prisoner suicide. This line of research is especially warranted because the improved understanding of the impact of affective states upon prisoner suicidality could inform future treatment developments, already progressing within the field of personality disorder (McMurran & Jinks, 2012). Indeed, the past decade has seen some progress within this field, with a growing number of pilot trials of psychological interventions for prisoners diagnosed with borderline personality disorder, both in the UK (Gee & Reed, 2013; Nee & Farman, 2008), the US (Berzins & Trestman, 2004; Black, Blum, McCormick, & Allen, 2013) and Australia (Eccleston & Sorbello, 2002). These trials have delivered variants of dialectical behaviour therapy (Linehan, 1993), a form of cognitive behaviour therapy that has proved to be effective in the alleviation of distress associated with emotional dysregulation. So far, results have been encouraging, including in terms of the reduction of self-harming behaviours by prisoner recipients. The efficacy of such interventions to the suicidal prisoner, who would not attract a diagnosis of borderline personality disorder, should also be investigated.

Therapy developments

This monograph has offered a summary of some recent treatment developments within the field of prisoner suicide prevention. Whilst preliminary findings will need to be confirmed within larger scale randomised controlled trials, there must continually be consideration of further treatment improvements. How can we make cognitive behaviour therapy for prisoners even better at reducing suicidality? Ideas presented earlier indicate how we could develop a more detailed understanding of the psychological mechanisms behind prisoner suicide, which could then form treatment targets. However, in addition to refining the *content* of the therapy, we should also consider the *process* of therapy, that is not just what should the therapy focus upon, but also how the therapy should be delivered. Chapter 4 presented a summary of the cognitive behavioural suicide prevention therapy recently piloted in a UK prison. This intervention was an individual therapy delivered once or twice weekly for up to four months. These parameters of delivery must be optimised.

For instance would a group therapy format be better received by prisoners? There may be a greater level of familiarity with group interventions amongst prisoners because many of the offending behaviour programmes are delivered on a group basis. Group interventions would allow for individuals to exchange stories and narratives of their own experiences of suicidality, which may normalise difficulties and helpfully undermine any appraisals that the prisoner is the 'only one feeling like this'. Also, a group format may enable social relationships and peer support to develop amongst participants in a relatively safe and protected setting. Through helping vulnerable others within the group, a participant may gain a renewed appreciation of his or her own value and what such helpful behaviour says about himself or herself as a person (i.e. social reciprocity). Also, the exchange of tips and advice on 'what worked for me' could be facilitated within the group, thus providing participants the opportunity to talk from a position of expertise by experience, rather than relying upon the therapist for having all the answers. Of course, group formats have their disadvantages, with group dynamic processes having to be carefully managed. Peer-to-peer relationships outside the group may already exist, which may then have an impact upon the dynamics and performance of the group. This issue may be more likely when participants are drawn from an 'enclosed population', such as a prison, compared with groups delivered within the general community when concurrent relationships amongst participants may be less likely. As with all therapy groups, confidentiality must be ensured, although this may prove challenging within a prison environment if knowledge of a prisoner's vulnerability could be used as currency to gain advantage over a fellow prisoner.

The tradition within psychotherapy of having a weekly session lasting for the 'therapy hour' may not be the most appropriate form of delivery within a prison setting. There is already some movement towards the development of 'intensive' treatments for anxiety disorders experienced by people living in the community (Ehlers et al., 2010; Oldfield, Salkovskis, & Taylor, 2011), and so this possibility should be explored within prisons. For instance an intensive therapy format may condense 20 therapeutic hours from a four-month therapy window into one week (i.e. four hours per day for five days). An intensive therapy format may help to overcome some of the constraints of a prison regime, such as the, oftentimes frustratingly, frequent occurrence of prisoners being unexpectedly transferred between prisons with little, if any, prior notice. Such transfers can occur during a four-month therapy window, leaving the prisoner with no opportunity to complete any ongoing work. Also, more intensive intervention formats could provide prisoners with an extended opportunity to engage in new cognitive processes and skills training. This opportunity is beginning to be explored within prison settings (e.g. Miles, Ellis, & Sheeran, 2012), although considerable further work is required to refine intensive cognitive behavioural therapy for prisoners.

As observed in Chapter 7, the delivery of psychological interventions within a prison setting can often require considerable modification. Several practical changes may need to be made to the treatment delivery to improve the 'fit' within the environment such as shorter sessions because of limited time available for healthcare interventions, increased drop-outs caused by unexpected transfers, restricted access to quality therapy rooms and so on. Perhaps one of the current challenges facing the clinician attempting to work with suicidal prisoners is the culture and attitude held amongst some prison staff that downplays the importance and sensitivity of mental health issues, such as suicidality. A lack of suicide awareness training and clinically informed supervision can contribute to the understanding of suicidal behaviour as 'manipulative' or 'attention-seeking'. Whilst understandable, this can be extremely unhelpful and serve to undermine an individual prisoner's progress during therapy. We argue that such attitudes should be better understood rather than dismissed. Prison officer attitudes and wing cultures represent further targets for intervention, especially if the focus of a suicide prevention programme is to move beyond the suicidal individual and towards a more systemic understanding. Prisoners exist in a highly iatrogenic environment and, therefore, the impact of the setting should be considered.

Chapter 5 offers one approach that may offer promise. Engaging prison officers in a psycho-education training programme would enable staff to develop skills in directly working with suicidal prisoners. In our experience of delivering therapy to individual prisoners, we have often been left with a clear impression that prison officers want to learn more about the intervention and wanted to contribute to a prisoner's recovery, if only they knew how. Staff training in problem-solving skills stands to not only benefit the suicidal prisoner, but also would allow for the development of alternative staff attitudes that suicidal behaviour is often a result of inescapable pain that the prisoner feels he or she has no other way of expressing. More adaptive attitudes held by staff coupled with a basic skill set in how best to support a vulnerable prisoner could then further contribute to the reduction of prisoner suicide – a goal that all staff and prisoners would share.

References

Afifi, T., Enns, M., Cox, B., Asmundson, G., Stein, M., & Sareen, J. (2008). Population attributable fractions of psychiatric disorders and suicide ideation and attempts associated with adverse childhood experiences. *American Journal of Public Health, 98*(5), 946–952.

Barton, J.J., Meade, T., Cumming, S., & Samuels, A. (2014). Predictors of self-harm in male inmates. *Journal of Criminal Psychology, 4*(1), 2–18.

Berzins, L.G., & Trestman, R.L. (2004). The development and implementation of dialectical behavior therapy in forensic settings. *International Journal of Forensic Mental Health, 3*(1), 93–103.

Birmingham, L. (2003). The mental health of prisoners. *Advances in Psychiatric Treatment, 9*, 191–201.

Black, D. W., Blum, N., McCormick, B., & Allen, J. (2013). Systems training for emotional predictability and problem solving (STEPPS) group treatment for offenders with borderline personality disorder. *The Journal of Nervous and Mental Disease, 201*(2), 124–129.

Cha, C. B., & Nock, M. K. (2009). Emotional intelligence is a protective factor for suicidal behavior. *Journal of the American Academy of Child & Adolescent Psychiatry, 48*(4), 422–430.

Ciarrochi, J., Deane, F. P., & Anderson, S. (2002). Emotional intelligence moderates the relationship between stress and mental health. *Personality and Individual Differences, 32*(2), 197–209.

Corcoran, P., Gallagher, J., Keeley, H. S., Arensman, E., & Perry, I .J. (2006). Adverse childhood experiences and lifetime suicide ideation: A cross-sectional study in a non-psychiatric hospital setting. *Irish Medical Journal, 99*(2), 42–45.

Csikszentmihalyi, M., & Larson, R. (1987). Validity and reliability of the experience – sampling method. *Journal of Nervous Mental Disorder, 175*, 526–536.

de Jong, M. L. (1992). Attachment, individuation, and risk of suicide in late adolescence. *Journal of Youth and Adolescence, 21*(3), 357–373.

Department of Health. (2001). *Safety first.* London, UK: Author.

Department of Health. (2002). *National suicide prevention strategy for England.* London, UK: Author.

Department of Health. (2009). *Improving access to psychological therapies: Offenders – positive practice guide.* London, UK: Author.

Department of Health. (2012). *Preventing suicide in England: A cross-government outcomes strategy to save lives.* London, UK: Author.

Department of Health. (2013). *Making mental health services more effective and accessible.* London, UK: Author.

Department of Health and HM Prison Service. (2002). *Developing and modernising primary care in prisons.* London, UK: Department of Health.

Dobson, K. S., & Khatri, N. (2000). Cognitive therapy: Looking backward, looking forward. *Journal of Clinical Psychology, 56*, 907–923.

Dube, S., Anda, R., Felitti, V., Chapman, D., Williamson, D., & Giles, W. (2001). Childhood abuse, household dysfunction, and the risk of attempted suicide throughout the life span. *Journal of the American Medical Association, 286*, 3089–3096.

Earthrowl, M., O'Grady, J., & Birmingham, L. (2003). Providing treatment to prisoners with mental disorders: Development of a policy. *British Journal of Psychiatry, 182*, 299–302.

Eccleston, L., & Sorbello, L. (2002). The RUSH program – Real Understanding of Self-Help: A suicide and self-harm prevention initiative within a prison setting. *Australian Psychologist, 37*(3), 237–244.

Ehlers, A., Clark, D. M., Hackmann, A., Grey, N., Liness, S., Wild, J., . . . McManus, F. (2010). Intensive cognitive therapy for PTSD: A feasibility study. *Behavioural and Cognitive Psychotherapy, 38*(4), 383–398.

Felthous, A. R. (2011). Suicide behind bars: Trends, inconsistencies, and practical implications. *Journal of Forensic Sciences, 56*, 1541–1555.

Gee, J., & Reed, S. (2013). The HoST programme: A pilot evaluation of modified dialectical behaviour therapy with female offenders diagnosed with borderline personality disorder. *European Journal of Psychotherapy & Counselling, 15*(3), 233–252.

Godet-Mardirossian, H., Jehel, L., & Falissard, B. (2011). Suicidality in male prisoners: Influence of childhood adversity mediated by dimensions of personality. *Journal of Forensic Sciences, 56*(4), 942–949.

Hammett, T.M., Gaiter, J.L., & Crawford, C. (1998). Reaching seriously at-risk populations: Health interventions in criminal justice settings. *Health Education & Behavior, 25*, 99–120.

HM Inspectorate of Prisons. (2014). HM *Chief Inspector of Prisons for England and Wales: Annual Report 2013–14.* London, UK: Author. Retrieved from www.justiceinspectorates.gov.uk/hmiprisons/wp-content/uploads/sites/4/2014/10/HMIP-AR_2013-14.pdf

Hughes, R.A. (2000). Health, place and British prisons. *Health & Place, 6*(1), 57–62.

Humber, N., Emsley, R., Pratt, D., & Tarrier, N. (2013). Anger as a predictor of psychological distress and self-harm ideation in inmates: A structured self-assessment diary study. *Psychiatry Research, 210*, 166–173.

Linehan, M.M. (1993). *Cognitive-behavioural treatment of borderline personality disorder.* New York, NY: Guilford Press.

Lipsey, M.W., Landenberger, N.A., & Wilson, S.J. (2007). Effects of cognitive behavioural programs for criminal offenders. *Campbell Systematic Reviews, 6*, 1–27.

Lizardi, D., Grunebaum, M.F., Burke, A., Stanley, B., Mann, J.J., Harkavy-Friedman, J., & Oquendo, M. (2011). The effect of social adjustment and attachment style on suicidal behaviour. *Acta Psychiatrica Scandinavica, 124*(4), 295–300.

Lynch, T.R., Cheavens, J.S., Morse, J.Q., & Rosenthal, M.Z. (2004). A model predicting suicidal ideation and hopelessness in depressed older adults: The impact of emotion inhibition and affect intensity. *Aging & Mental Health, 8*(6), 486–497.

McDougall, C., Perry, A.E., Clarbour, J., Bowles, R., & Worthy, G. (2009). *Evaluation of HM Prison Service enhanced thinking skills programme: Report on the outcomes from a randomised controlled trial* (Ministry of Justice Research Series 3/09). London, UK: Ministry of Justice.

McMurran, M., & Jinks, M. (2012). Making your emotions work for you: A pilot brief intervention for alexithymia with personality-disordered offenders. *Personality and Mental Health, 6*, 45–49.

Miles, H.L., Ellis, K., & Sheeran, A.E. (2012). 'Coping inside?': The prevalence of anxiety and OCD amongst incarcerated young offenders and an evaluation of a one-day CBT workshop. *Journal of Forensic Psychiatry & Psychology, 23*(5–6), 689–705.

Nee, C., & Farman, S. (2008). Treatment of borderline personality disorder in prisons: Findings from the two dialectical behaviour therapy pilots in the UK. In J.C. Hagen & E.I. Jensen (Eds.), *Personality disorders: New research* (pp. 107–121). New York, NY: Nova Science.

Oldfield, V.B., Salkovskis, P.M., & Taylor, T. (2011). Time-intensive cognitive behaviour therapy for obsessive-compulsive disorder: A case series and matched comparison group. *British Journal of Clinical Psychology, 50*(1), 7–18.

Palmier-Claus, J.E., Myin-Germeys, I., Barkus, E., Bentley, L., Udachina, A., Delespaul, P.A., . . . Dunn, G. (2011). Experience sampling research in individuals with mental illness: Reflections and guidance. *Acta Psychiatrica Scandinavica, 123*, 12–20.

Singleton, N., Meltzer, H., & Gatward, R. (1998). *Psychiatric morbidity among prisoners*. London, UK: Stationery Office.

Tarrier, N., Gooding, P., Pratt, D., Kelly, J., Awenat, Y., & Maxwell, J. (2013). *Cognitive behavioural prevention of suicide in psychosis: A treatment manual*. London, UK: Routledge.

Travis, A. (2015, January 22). Prison suicide rate at highest level since 2007, figures show. *The Guardian*. Retrieved from http://www.theguardian.com/society/2015/jan/22/prison-suicide-rate-82-deaths

Wilson, D. B., Bouffard, L. A., & Mackenzie, D. L. (2005). A quantitative review of structured, group-oriented, cognitive-behavioral programs for offenders. *Criminal Justice and Behavior, 32*(2), 172–204.

World Health Organization. (2014). *Prisons and health*. Retrieved from http://www.euro.who.int/en/health-topics/health-determinants/prisons-and-health/publications/2014/prisons-and-health

Index

Note: Page numbers in *italics* indicate figures and tables.

adjustment process in prison 41, 108–9
adverse childhood experiences and suicide risk 137–8
age and prison suicide 20
appointments, importance of keeping 125–6
appraisal restructuring 56
Assessment, Care in Custody and Teamwork (ACCT) initiative 13–14, 59, 69–70, 76, 77
assessment for CBSP 53–4
attentional control training 55–6
availability, importance of 122–3
average daily population (ADP) of inmates 6

behavioural activation 57–8
Bradley Report 133
Broaden & Build principles 53
Broad Minded Affecting Coping (BMAC) technique 53, 55–6

case example: of CBSP 60–4, *62*; of PST 77–81
case formulation for CBSP 54, *62*
CBSP *see* Cognitive Behavioural Suicide Prevention (CBSP) therapy
CBT *see* cognitive behavior therapy
challenges of implementation: contextual 104–8, 133, 135; engagement 123–8; exits 128–9; implications for research practice 130–1; individual 108–11; overview 103–4, 113; recruitment 119–23
choice, offering 127

clinical risk factors: history of suicidal behaviour 23–5; personality disorder 31–2; psychiatric diagnoses and contact with mental health care services 25–8; substance use 29–30
cognitive behaviour therapy (CBT): focus of 136; for suicidality 51–2; tailoring delivery for prison environment 112
Cognitive Behavioural Suicide Prevention (CBSP) therapy: appraisal restructuring 56; attentional control training 55–6; behavioural activation 57–8; case example 60–4, *62*; delivery of 53, 107, 108; engagement and assessment 53–4; maintaining well-being plans 58; overview 52–3, 64–5; preliminary results for 59–60; problem-solving skills training 56–7; schema-focused techniques 58; treatment 54
'collateral damage' from suicide attempts 134
commitment to work of prison 104
community engagement approach to recruitment 119–23
co-morbidity of psychiatric diagnoses 37, 133
confidentiality 111, 123–5
contact, barriers to maintaining 125–6, 129
contextual challenges to implementation 104–8, 133, 135
continuum of suicide 3, 40
Cooksey, David 98
coping skills, perceptions of 42, *43*

countries: male prisoners in 7; rates of suicide in 4
Cry of Pain model 38–9
custodial status, as risk factor 21

defeat, perceptions of 39, 41–2, *43*, 57
delivery: of CBSP 53, 107, 108; tailoring for prison environment 112; of therapy 105–6; *see also* research study on delivery of psychological therapy
demographic risk factors 19–21
diagnostic models of suicide, psychological models contrasted with 36–8
dialectical behaviour therapy 139
directions for future research: theory developments 136–9; therapy developments 139–41
Durkheim, E. 2, 4

emotional regulation and suicide risk 138–9
engagement: in studies 123–8; in therapeutic programmes 105, 109–10
entrapment, perceptions of 39, 41–2, *43*, 57
evaluation study 115
exiting research 128–9
experience sampling methodology 137

feasibility studies 75–6, 81, 115, 135–6; *see also* forensic service user involvement; Prevention of Suicide in Prisons (PROSPeR) study
forensic service user involvement: activities 93–7; challenges 97; group meetings 89–90; impact 97–9; other opportunities for involvement 99; overview 86, 99–100; purpose of 86–7; recruitment process 87–8; role of consultants 88–9; training and support needs 90–3

gatekeeper approach to recruitment 118, 119
gender and prison suicide 7, 20
Glover, R. M. 5
goals for CBSP, identifying 54
gossip culture 95
group therapy interventions 139–40

healthcare, access to 64–5
history: of alcohol drug abuse or dependence, as risk factor 29–30; of psychiatric contact, as risk factor 25–8; of suicidal behaviour, as risk factor 23–5
HM Prison Service: Assessment, Care in Custody and Teamwork (ACCT) initiative of 13–14, 59, 69–70, 76, 77; suicide prevention and 12–13
homework tasks 94–5, 110–11
hopelessness 39, 57

illiteracy 110–11, 121, 125
implementation challenges: challenges of implementation 119–23; contextual 104–8, 133, 135; engagement 123–8; exits 128–9; implications for research practice 130–1; individual 108–11; overview 103–4, 113
'imported vulnerability', interaction with 'relational dimensions' 49–50
incentives, use of 121–2
individual challenges to implementation 108–11
induction, recruitment at 120
informed consent 123–4
Integrated Motivational Volitional model 40
intensive therapy format 140
International Association for Suicide Prevention Task Force on Suicide in Prisons 11
Interpersonal Theory 39, 44
interviews of suicidal prisoners 117
involvement in research 85

jails in US 5, 9
Joiner, Thomas 39

length of sentence, as risk factor 22
Listener prisoners 116–17, 120
literacy rates 110–11, 121, 125

male prisoner suicide, numbers and rates of 7
manipulative: motives for self-harm viewed as 24; prisoners viewed as 107, 141
marital status and prison suicide 20–1

medical diagnostic models of suicide, psychological models contrasted with 36–8
Medical Research Council 98
medications, and suicidal thoughts and behaviours 37–8
mental health care services: access to 134; previous contact with, as risk factor 25–8
mental health problems: identification of 64; personality disorder 31–2, 139; prevalence of 133; stigma of 94–5, 106; *see also* psychiatric diagnoses
Mental Health Research Network 91
misclassification of suicides 4, 6
Motivational Interviewing 110

National Suicide Prevention Strategy for England 103

offence type, as risk factor 23
outcomes of CBSP 60

pain, habituation to 39
participation in research 85
Patient and Public Involvement (PPI) 85, 98–9; *see also* Service User Reference Groups
personality disorder, as risk factor 31–2, 139
prevention of suicide in prisons: overview 11–14; theoretical approach to 35–6; *see also* Cognitive Behavioural Suicide Prevention (CBSP) therapy; problem-solving therapy; risk factors
Prevention of Suicide in Prisons (PROSPeR) study 59, 86, 115
primary prevention strategies 50
prisoners: awareness of dangers to 109; key events in life of 108; as manipulative or attention-seeking 107, 141; *see also* rates of suicide
'prison mask' 109
prison population rate 1
prison suicide, definition 5–6
prison systems: healthcare within 133; structures of 5; in US 5, 9; wing culture of 105; *see also* HM Prison Service; suicidal behaviour in prisons
problem-solving skills training in CBSP 56–7

problem-solving therapy (PST): benefits of 70; case example 77–81; decision making 80; generating solutions 79–80; implementation of in prisons 75–6; intervention 76–7; overview 81; recognising and identifying problems 79; results of research on 71–2, *73*, 74–5; SMART action plan 81; theoretical basis underlying 70–1
professionalisation and service user involvement 90–1
PROSPeR (Prevention of Suicide in Prisons) study 59, 86, 115
PST *see* problem-solving therapy
psychiatric diagnoses: co-morbidity of 37, 133; as risk factor 25–8; *see also* mental health problems
psychological interventions: directions for future research on 139–41; experience with 109; for prisoners 49–51; for suicidality 51–2; *see also* Cognitive Behavioural Suicide Prevention (CBSP) therapy; implementation challenges; problem-solving therapy; research study on delivery of psychological therapy
psychological models of suicide: application in prison setting 41–4; Cry of Pain 38–9; diagnostic models contrasted with 36–8; Integrated Motivational Volitional 40; Interpersonal Theory 39; need for 35–6; Schematic Appraisals 40–1

rapport, establishing 123, 127–8; *see also* therapeutic relationship
rates of suicide: in Australian prisoner population 9, 11; in general population 3–4; in prisoner population 6–7, *7*, *8*, 9, 11; in US prisoner population 9, *10*
recruitment: for forensic service user involvement 87–8; into studies 117–23
'relational dimensions', interaction with 'imported vulnerability' 49–50
release of prisoners during treatment 107
research study on delivery of psychological therapy: background 115–17; design *116*; engagement during studies 123–8; exiting studies

128–9; issues for planning and approving 130; recruitment into studies 117–23
retrospective methods, limitations of 137
risk factors: adverse childhood experiences 137–8; clinical 23–32; demographic 19–21; emotional regulation 138–9; limitations of prevention based on 35–6; situational 21–3
risk information, disclosure of 111

Samaritans 116
schema-focused techniques 58
Schematic Appraisals Model of Suicide (SAMS) 40–1, 44, 52, 55, 56
secondary prevention strategies 50
self-harm: definition 3; manipulative motives in 24; prevalence of 69
self-inflicted deaths (SIDs) 5–6, *8*
sentence length, as risk factor 22
service user involvement 85
Service User Reference Groups (SURGs): activities 93–7; challenges 97; definition 85–6; forensic 86–7; impact 97–9; meetings 89–90; other opportunities for involvement 99; overview 99–100; as participants in focus group 115–16; recruitment process 87–8; role of 88–9; training and support needs 90–3
situational risk factors 21–3
socially excluded population 49, 134
social support, perceptions of 43–4
staff, psycho-education training programme for 141; *see also* problem-solving therapy
stigma: of mental health conditions 94–5, 106; of prison suicide 6; of weakness 120–1

substance use, as risk factor 29–30
suicidal behaviour in prisons: defined 11; as manipulative and attention-seeking 107, 141; prevalence of 133–4; psychological mechanisms of 135
suicide: continuum of 3, 40; definition 1–3; misclassification of 4, 6; *see also* psychological models of suicide; rates of suicide; risk factors
Suicide Prevention Strategies for England 134
SURGs *see* Service User Reference Groups

terminology and vocabulary, use of 94–5, 109–10, 118
theoretical approach, importance of 35, 136–9
therapeutic relationship: establishing 105, 109; risk information disclosure and 111; *see also* rapport, establishing
time in custody, as risk factor 21–2
translation gaps in application of research findings 98
treatment options, evidence for 70
type of offence, as risk factor 23

Understanding the Psychology of Suicide (UPSide) research group 37, 38, 52

weakness, showing 120–1
well-being plan, maintaining 58
Williams, Mark 38–9
wing culture of prisons 105
withdrawal: from drugs or alcohol, as risk factor 30; from therapy 106
workshop spaces, access to 106
written tasks between therapy sessions 94–5, 110–11